MW01195986

PERFECT
NEEDLEPOINT
PROJECTS
from start to finish

PERFECT NEEDLEPOINT PROJECTS

from start to finish

KATHERINE B. ARCHER
AND
PATRICIA FALK FEELEY

ST. MARTIN'S PRESS   NEW YORK

Copyright © 1977 by Katherine B. Archer and Patricia Falk Feeley
All rights reserved
For information, write:
  St. Martin's Press
  175 Fifth Avenue
  New York, N.Y. 10010

Manufactured in the United States of America
Library of Congress Catalog Card Number: 75-40786

Library of Congress Cataloging in Publication Data

Archer, Katherine B
  Perfect needlepoint projects from start to finish.

Bibliography: p.
Includes index.
1. Canvas embroidery.   I. Feeley, Patricia Falk,
joint author.   II. Title.
TT778.C3A73   746.4′4   75-40786

ISBN 0-312-60070-4

For Bob, who is proud of me.

K.B.A.

For my mother, who is patient, and Molly, who is a nice child.

P.F.F.

CONTENTS

APPENDICES

FOREWORD

In a sense, this book began on a snowy night some five years ago, on a broken-down commuter train between Pat Feeley's office in New York and her home in Darien, Connecticut. Pat decided, then and there, to take up something that would pass the hours of traveling (or not traveling, as was all too often the case); since she had never cared much for poker or bridge, she chanced on needlepoint, and has been at it ever since. Kathy Archer took up needlepoint, after trying her hand at knitting and embroidery and watching friends needlepoint madly, finally deciding that there must be something to it—and so there is.

We had both, at times, dreaded the completion of stitching on a piece, for we never knew quite what to do then.

Needlepoint is heavy and hard to sew; early on, we ruined a couple of pieces with amateur finishing jobs. After that we began having work professionally finished. That proved to be so time-consuming that we grew notorious for late Christmas and birthday gifts, so expensive that we balked at spending $35 or so to complete something that had cost perhaps $5 in materials, and so unsatisfactory that we would occasionally have to pick something apart and put it together again closer to the way we'd wanted it in the first place. We joined forces to write this book since we had both struggled with similar problems and wanted to share our solutions with you.

There were then no books at all on blocking and finishing; the instructions in most needlepoint books were too vague to help us produce anything but the most lumpy and homemade-looking objects. So we decided to learn to do blocking and finishing that would have a professional look at little expense. Working our way from the simple to the complex, correcting our own disasters as we went, and trying a good many things that we frankly thought would not succeed, we ended up, we think, with something worth sharing. Some other books will teach you stitchery and design; this one will give you an idea of what you can make and how to go about making what you want, whether you are an expert or just starting out.

A glance through the illustrations will show you what is here. We hope the book will provide both inspiration and instruction and that it will help make a useful and pleasurable hobby even more pleasant for its readers.

KATHY ARCHER
PAT FEELEY

PERFECT NEEDLEPOINT PROJECTS
from start to finish

1

CHE BASICS

Perhaps it is obvious, but we've too often missed the point ourselves to let it pass. The very first step in needlepoint—as in all handwork—is to decide, even before you purchase your materials, what you want to make. That decision will determine what your materials should be and what approach will give the most satisfactory results. Consider where you'll be working; you'll want a small, portable project if you travel a good deal, while a larger project that can be left on a standing frame might be best if you're housebound during a long winter.

Perhaps, for instance, you want to make a backgammon board. To avoid the expense of time-consuming custom work when you've finished your stitch-

ing, check the mail-order section of this book, inquire of the firms that make trays for backgammon boards, order what you want directly or through a local shop, and have the tray in hand before you plan the dimensions of your board on canvas. Decide either on using stitches that minimize canvas distortion or on using a frame; either way, you want your finished piece to fit perfectly into the tray you've planned it for.

Work out your design, purchase your canvas and yarns, transfer your design to canvas, prepare the canvas, and set to work. When you've finished stitching you'll be ready—with a minimum of blocking and sizing—to turn the margins of your canvas, catch-stitch them to the back of the

1

needlepoint, slip-stitch your backing into place, and set your piece into the board.

This is certainly a more satisfactory procedure than picking out a piece because it takes your fancy, working on it, and then stowing it away in a drawer for months because you don't really know what to do with it.

Part of doing things the right way, of course, is measuring. A belt, a case for your scissors, a vest for your husband—whatever it is, measure first. After all, no belt, however lovely, is quite a success if it's too long or too short or if its buckle was bought merely to fit the piece rather than to enhance it. Unless you're lucky, a vest for which you've neglected to make and fit a muslin pattern first will make a man look like a scarecrow or a sausage, no matter how beautiful the design or the stitching may be. Even a scissors case is a failure if you must rummage the stores for a pair that will slip into it. The basic steps are surprisingly easy to neglect; once neglected, the trials to one's temper are considerable. Decide first, measure first, and your pleasure in your needlework will be much enhanced.

Picking Your Canvas

Plain Canvas

Canvas is the basic medium for all needlepoint. The mesh number indicates the number of meshes to the running inch, and canvas comes in sizes from 40 mesh, called gauze, used for petit point, to 3 mesh rug canvas. Some canvases have special purposes, and these days canvas comes in a wide variety of different textures, weights, and weaves.

In choosing a canvas, remember that fine canvas is most suited to small projects, large-mesh canvas to larger ones. In addition, consider your time; working in continental stitch on 18 mesh canvas demands almost four times as many stitches to the square inch as it would on 10 mesh canvas. Consider also the amount of detail your design will call for. The finer the canvas, the more detail you can work into your design.

Canvas comes by the yard, just like fabric. If it is seriously off grain (that is, if the horizontal and vertical threads are not at right angles), cut the selvages away, straighten the canvas, pin it into place, and press it with a warm steam iron.

Plain-weave monocanvas comes in mesh sizes 24, 18, 16, 14, 12, and 10, in widths up to 54 inches for the larger sizes and up to 40 inches for the smaller ones. It should be sized so that it is stiff and shiny, not powdery. Don't ever buy canvas of any type that has threads that have been broken and retied; these threads could break under the stress of blocking or use. Monocanvas comes in white and brown; the white is best for painting designs.

Bargello monocanvas comes in one one mesh size, 13, which takes a full strand of Persian wool in bargello and a single thread doubled over for the continental or diagonal stitch. It is made of rough jute fiber, which holds the long bargello stitches in place better than does the regular cotton monocanvas. Bargello canvas is wiry and resilient, and its color is brown.

Interlock monocanvas, fairly new on the market, comes in 10, 12, and 14 mesh. It looks like monocanvas at first glance, but it's lock-woven for extra sturdiness and stability. It is excellent for general use, lends itself to designing just as well as regular monocanvas, and has but two mild drawbacks. The first is that it is sized with what seems to be a stiff, snaggy finish, which is hard on the hands and on knit fabrics—including stockings. The second is that despite its double-thread construction, it does not allow the working of petit point detail.

Penelope canvas comes in 5, 7, 8, 10, 12, 14, 16, 18, and 20 mesh sizes; the large meshes come in widths up to 54 inches, the smaller in widths up to 40 inches. Because of its double-thread construction, you can separate the threads to do petit point detail, to make 20 mesh from the 10, and so on. The construction also permits the use of the half-cross stitch for pieces that won't receive heavy wear. Penelope is generally more flexible than monocanvas of the same mesh size.

Some people find it confusing to work with, though we don't; however, it is more difficult to paint on if you do your own designs. Unless you want to use it sideways for a special effect, it doesn't work well for bargello. Unlike monocanvas, which can be stitched with the top of the work lined up in either direction, penelope should be worked with the selvages at the sides.

Jacquard canvas seems to be available in a good many shops. It is an 8-mesh, very sturdy canvas with a complicated weave that makes a design in two colors. It takes a full strand of Persian wool very well. Patterns include a scallop shell, a fleur-de-lis, a snowflake, and others; with an imaginative use of color, results with it can be most attractive. For rugs, center the design carefully, allow ample margins, and devise a border. Buy it by the piece or by the yard; it comes 54 inches wide.

Rug canvas comes in 3, 4, and 5 mesh sizes, up to 60 inches wide. It is used for rugs and for the so-called quick point stitch with rug rool or several strands of Persian. We cannot abide it and use large penelope for rugs in its stead. Real rug canvas is immensely stiff and harsh, difficult to work with, and apt to take the skin right off your hands. If you use it, buy a pair of night gloves at the drugstore and cut off the fingertips for your stitching hand. Leave 4 or 5 inches all around for blocking.

Kits and painted or silk-screened canvases are available in wide variety from local and mail-order sources. Some supply only the wool to complete the stitching, others all the materials to complete the project. You can spend from $2.50 for a patch for your blue jeans to several hundred dollars for a large, lovely custom rug. The best rule of thumb, however, is to stick to good-quality things that come with an ample supply of Persian wool; they will stand up best and repay the time and effort you put into them. Specialty shops will prepare a design to your specifications; for an appropriate (and substantial) amount, they will paint the canvas and supply the wool for whatever project you have in mind.

Partially preworked canvases are available in every art-needlework department or shop. Some of them are hideous old things—cabbage roses, dismal colors—but more and more the designs are becoming attractive and contemporary. Most are done in tapestry wool on 10-mesh penelope, and all you need do is pick a background stitch and enough tapestry wool to fill in the background and go to work. Pictures, brick covers for doorstops, luggage straps—all manner of things are available. You can adapt a pillow or picture for a handsome tote, by using several coordinated pieces of the same for a pieced rug, or whatever imagination presents. Partially preworked canvases are particularly good beginner projects.

Prefinished or Premounted Items are fairly new on the market, and the list of available pieces is growing longer all the time. Coasters, cushions, typewriter covers, watchbands, tennis-racket jackets and totes; handbags, pillows, French purses and purse accessories; checkbook covers, eyeglass cases and key cases; luggage tags, photo albums; covers for telephone directories, address books, magazine racks, Lucite ice buckets, and cachepots; wastebaskets and desk sets for needlepoint inserts; gameboards, belts, golf-club covers— are among the items offered by a variety of companies listed in the mail-order section. All of the things that these firms offer would present some difficulty in finishing at home, and most are quite costly to have finished professionally, so we wholeheartedly recommend their use.

All are assembled, most with 12 mesh interlock monocanvas that folds or zips free for working. You can paint your design, if you wish, and you can use bargello, continental, or basketweave stitch for it, though you are confined mainly to the use of stitches that will not pull the canvas out of shape, since it's impossible to unmount, block, and remount a piece that has become distorted.

Most premounted things come in a reasonable range of colors, but if you want something different, try your hand at making your own premounted items. You'll find the catalogs of the major pattern companies helpful; check them for patterns for dolls and stuffed animals adaptable to needlepoint, for clothing patterns, and for embroidery layouts that you can use on canvas.

MEDIA OTHER THAN TRUE CANVAS

Plastic canvas, made in a variety of shapes and sizes by Columbia-Minerva, is sold as Hi-Straw Perforated Plastic and Needlepoint FashionEase canvas. Much as we dislike anything made of plastic, we find this to be very convenient stuff, for you need not prepare it, block it, or worry about raveling. You can trim it with scissors or a mat knife to the shape you want, finish it easily with a binding stitch, and stitch small pieces together to make larger objects. It's unsurpassed as a medium for beginners to work on, though designs must be counted off, since painting on it is impossible. It is most probably a derivation of the wonderful, old-fashioned perforated cards on which generations of girls learned their first cross stitch.

Blank perforated cards are hard to find in shops but can be obtained by mail. They are good for simple cross stitch but also adapt themselves well to more sophisticated pictures and samplers. They do not require a background, and you work as you would on any needlepoint canvas, with special attention to keeping a loose tension, so as to avoid buckling or tearing the card.

Fabrics lend themselves to a variety of needlework. Even-weave linens and wools, worked with the aid of a frame, are good media for cross stitch, needlepoint stitches, or, most particularly, for bargello. Try them with crewel wool and crewel needles. The result can then be used in anything—garment, curtain, whatever—that might ordinarily be made from fabric of the same weight. Mark out pattern pieces as if you were going to work with fabric alone, but do not cut them out until you've completed your stitchery; then proceed with the usual sewing directions for your pattern.

It is also possible to do needlepoint through canvas onto a backing fabric, and then to pull the canvas threads out with pliers, leaving the needlepoint design on a fabric background, usually velvet or wool. To do this, you must use canvas stretchers, over which both backing fabric and canvas are stretched tightly and evenly. Practically speaking, this limits the size of your project to that of a picture or fire screen. Work with a stabbing motion, up and down, with one hand below the canvas and one above to send the needle back and forth; this will assure even stitching and a good result. We wouldn't advise this for anything that will receive heavy wear.

Original designing:

If you've worked only from kits or painted canvas, try making an object that will be wholly original and wholly yours. Start with a simple project, such as a monogrammed eyeglass case that you can work out first on graph paper, a child's drawing that you can trace right onto the canvas, or a Christmas stocking with a simple design adapted from a decoration or greeting card.

You can also work from other types of cards, from wallpaper, book illustrations, prints and drawings—anything, really, that takes your fancy. You can get your models to the right size by enlarging them photostatically, by the graph method, or with the aid of one or another of the ruled overlays now on the market.

If you wish to paint your canvas rather than counting off the stitches from a graph, first trace the outlines of your design onto the canvas. Then use waterproof felt-tip markers, well-thinned acrylic paints, or oil paints thinned down with turpentine and a bit of japan drier. The paint should be the consistency of cream, thin enough not to clog the meshes. If you make an error, paint it out with a bit of white. You can also use ordinary wax crayons; a box of 64 colors is inexpensive, and we all remember just how to use them. Set the colors by ironing between two sheets of brown paper.

You may choose to trace your outlines onto canvas and not to paint at all if your color scheme is a bold one without shading. This can be a pleasant way of working.

No matter what you use to paint your canvas, spray it with a thin, clear acrylic spray to keep colors from running when the canvas is dampened for blocking or sprayed with a soil-repellent finish.

The commercial pattern companies that make dress patterns also make many crafts patterns that can be very helpful to the needlepointer. We recommend the use of these patterns for pillows, vests, totes, purses, and stuffed animals, among others. They can be a great source of ideas, and you should look in the crafts sections of the catalogs to see if you can adapt any of the patterns to needlepoint. For example, one of the companies has a pattern for a tennis tote bag with a racket jacket built into one side. It might look great if you made up the tote in canvas and the jacket panel in needlepoint. Use your imagination and take advantage of these great inventions.

PREPARING YOUR CANVAS

Pin the canvas out flat, with the selvages at the sides. Trace the outline of your project with pencil or a waterproof felt-tip marker. If it is part of something that will be pieced, such as rug squares, you'll have to work thread by thread so that the edges will match. For an irregular shape, allow enough canvas all around to make a rectangle that leaves two-inch margins from the edge of the canvas to the nearest line of stitching.

The graph method of enlarging. The tracing on the left was made on 8-square-to-the-inch paper. The enlargement on the right was made by repeating the tracing, square by square, onto 4-square-to-the-inch paper. If you are making a pair of something—slippers, the two sides of a vest, the front and back of a handbag—lay them out side by side, four inches apart. If

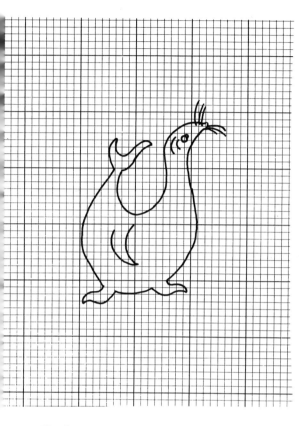

THE GRAPH METHOD OF ENLARGING

(DRAWINGS REDUCED FROM ORIGINALS)

Seal 1
8 squares to the inch

Seal 2
4 squares to the inch

you are making a set—rug squares, chair seats, upholstery, even coasters— use canvas from a single roll. For something like a bargello vest, stitch the foundation line of your design on both sections so that the pattern will match precisely at the center. You may then cut the pieces apart.

When you've marked your stitching outline and margins, cut out the canvas, fold between two threads about a half inch in from the cut edge on each side, press down firmly with your fingers or lightly with an iron, and stitch down with the zigzag stitch on your sewing machine. Always stitch parallel edges in the same direction to avoid distorting the canvas. A stitched edge will hold up much better, especially in blocking, than one bound in masking tape. If you are using a particularly harsh and snaggy canvas, you might want to bind the folded and stitched edges in tape or even sewn-down cotton bias binding to keep them from scraping your hands and snagging both the yarn and your clothing.

Mark the center mesh with a dot of color, and note original measurements in the margins for use in blocking and in cutting backing fabric later on.

Choosing Yarns

No matter what yarn you choose, estimate carefully the amount you will need by testing your stitches for a couple of square inches on the canvas you intend to use. If you find, for instance, that a yard of Persian wool, cut in two pieces for working, will cover 1¼ square inches of canvas if done in basket-weave stitch on 10 mesh monocanvas, you can figure out easily what it would take to cover a square 10 inches by 10 inches.

Figure our approximately how many square inches of each color are in your design (a piece of transparent graph paper or plastic will help you calculate for odd shapes), figure out what that means in yards, and purchase accordingly. With bargello patterns it is easier to figure each color as a percentage of the total design, to figure the amount of yarn for the whole piece, and then to figure your total amounts as

$$\frac{1 \text{ yard}}{1.25 \text{ square inches}} = \frac{\times \text{ yards}}{100 \text{ square inches}}$$

$$\frac{1 \text{ yard} \times 100}{1.25} = \times \text{ yards}$$

$$\frac{100 \text{ yards}}{1.25} = 80 \text{ yards}$$

percentage of the whole. There are about 40 yards to the ounce of Persian wool, so purchase accordingly. Always buy a bit more yarn than you think you'll need, and because dye lots differ slightly, always buy all the background yarn for a given project at the same time and from the same dye lot.

The supposed advantage of a kit, of course, is that the yarn is calculated accurately, but too often this is not the case. You should certainly complain to both retailer and manufacturer if a kit that you purchase proves to be short of yarn.

TYPES OF YARN

Persian wool is the most adaptable yarn for needlepoint and bargello. It is a fine, 3-strand yarn that comes in the widest possible selection of colors. The strands can easily be separated, and you use as many strands as the canvas demands, from one for petit point to six or more for rug canvas. There are many brands, though Paterna seems preferable for its sheen and for its depth and variety of color—nearly 350. There is a new acrylic version of this, too.

A few brands come only in 1-ounce skeins, but others offer a skein of about 9 yards and 2- and 4-ounce hanks. Some shops, however, sell all Persian wool by the ounce, allowing you to make up your purchase from several different colors. This is the most economical and waste-free way to buy your wool, and a shop that sells it this way is worth patronizing for the economy and flexibility it offers you.

Tapestry wool is a sturdy, tightly twisted yarn good for filling in backgrounds on preworked canvases. It fits 10 mesh penelope or 12 mesh monocanvases and can be used for bargello on 16 mesh canvas. The range of colors is smaller than that of Persian, and the colors are not as deep or as vivid.

Rug wool resembles fatter, rougher tapestry wool. Pass up any that breaks easily; it won't hold up. Generally we avoid synthetic yarns such as rayon or acrylic, though they are certainly the right choice for anything—such as a bathroom rug, or pillows for use on a boat or at a seaside house—that must be washable. Shops that stock Paterna Persian will order Paternayan rug wools for you if they do not have them in stock.

Crewel wool is a fine embroidery wool that can be used like Persian, one or two strands at a time, on petit point canvas. The color range is excellent.

Ver à soie silk comes in small 7-strand skeins in an extraordinary range of beautiful colors. It is imported, and very expensive, and consequently seems to be stocked by very few shops. One or two threads at a time will fit the finest petit point gauze, but the full strand works nicely on fine canvas for small things such as pincushions. You can use a bit for detail or accent in working with wool. Since it's all too easy to stain silk in blocking, and since it will not take steaming or high heat, make sure that you do not distort the canvas on which it is being worked, and use a low setting on your iron, a press cloth, and no moisture when you're finishing it.

Embroidery cotton comes in small hanks of six strands; the color range is excellent and the colors are fast in hot water. The yarn is good and for small items, and it's rather shiny look is attractive for detail. It also provides textural variation on larger items.

Metallic yarns, in a range of silver, gold, copper, and pewter tones, might appeal to you, especially for ecclesiastical work. Use several strands, experimenting to see what fits your canvas, and a larger needle than would be usual for the canvas. Wax the yarn ends slightly with beeswax—available where sewing supplies are sold—to minimize raveling. Metallic threads are best for accent. If you use them this way in a canvas done mostly in wool, stitch them in after blocking; if they make up a substantial part of the design, use a frame. These threads will tarnish if exposed to dampness in blocking or cleaning and may discolor just from the moisture and oil in your hands as you work. Not many shops carry them, but they are available by mail. Just for fun you may want to try what a friend of ours did. She used ordinary window screening and metallic thread to do some pictures derived from old botanical prints, and they were stunning.

Knitting and novelty yarns may be unorthodox for needlepoint, but they are readily available, come in interesting sizes and textures, and can be fun to experiment with for things that won't receive a great deal of wear. Use a very loose tension in stitching with them.

Knitting worsted just fits 10 mesh monocanvas for continental stitch; the acrylic sort is perfect for, say, a fancy patch for washable blue jeans. Mohair, with its deep colors and fluffy texture, would make a nice bargello vest; the judicious use of a wire dog brush will keep it fluffy and fresh. Some of the rough tweeds would fit rug canvas.

Whatever you want to try, experiment first with a few yards of wool on a scrap of the canvas you intend to use. Stitch, dampen, block, and see what happens. If your sample works out, your project will too. Try jute, raffia, cord—anything that appeals to you.

COLOR AND COLOR SCHEMES

If you have trouble choosing a color scheme, take a look at the color wheel. The primary colors are red, yellow, and blue. Red combines with yellow to make orange, yellow with blue to make green, blue with red to make purple. Further steps of color are between. Yellow is opposite purple, red opposite green, and blue opposite orange; shades are arrived at by adding black or gray to the basic colors of the wheel, and tints are achieved by adding white. Black is a combination of all the primaries, and white is the absence of all color.

You may work in tints and shades of one color. Or pick colors opposite one another on the wheel—flowers in shades and tints of red, for instance, and foliage in shades and tints of green. Or you can use colors adjacent to one another on the wheel, such as yellow, orange, and red.

Or adjacent colors plus an accent in an opposite color—blue and green with a dash of orange. Or in the so-called neutrals—the range of grays from white to black, the range of browns from cream to bitter chocolate—with accent colors; the result might be a combination of powder blue and bitter chocolate, or shades of gray with a gold accent.

A fabric that you really like will provide a good guide to the professional use of color; that wonderful print dress with the monarch butterflies and green ferns on the white ground provides you with a color scheme you can transmit successfully to needlepoint. As you lay out hanks of yarn to prepare for your canvas, those colors will fall together perfectly.

The best single piece of advice we've ever received about the use of color came from a decorator friend of ours and here it is: Never use any color that doesn't look good next to either black or white. If it doesn't, it lacks definition, depth, and vividness.

Useful tip: Avoid red, black, and snow white when making needlepoint to be used in garments.

Useful tip: If you are making something for a boat or a house at the shore be sure to use acrylic knitting worsted or the new acrylic Persian wool because it won't mildew.

YOUR OTHER TOOLS:

Scissors and Shears: A pair of sharp embroidery scissors for cutting single lengths of wool, trimming tag ends from the back of the work, and doing occasional picking out is a basic requirement. We also keep a special pair of tiny cuticle scissors and a pair of tweezers for picking out. The slender points and slight curve in the blade of the scissors make it easier to cut out a stitch at a time without risking a cut through the canvas thread, and the tweezers permit the pulling out of the cut stitch without damage to the alignment of the canvas.

Scissors etc.

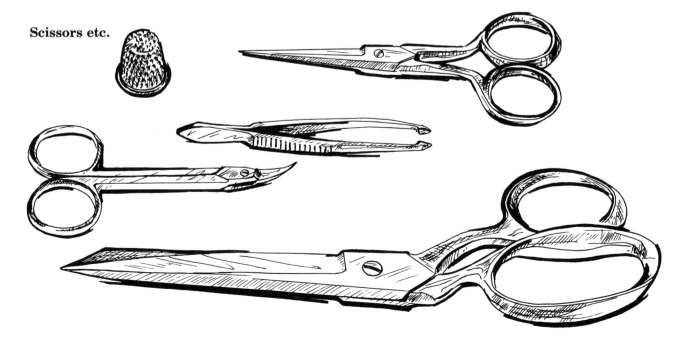

You'll also need a pair of sturdy shears for cutting canvas, heavy backing fabrics, and hanks of wool, and a pair of sharp sewing scissors for trimming backing, grading seam allowances, and other small tasks.

Thimbles: A thimble should fit your middle finger loosely. If you've done without one so far, try until you get the hang of using one; it will prevent your piercing your finger, or the alternative, developing an ugly callous. Buy the ordinary cheap metal thimble; the decorative ones are pretty but not efficient.

Needles: The "needle" in needlepoint is blunt rather than sharp, with a long, wide eye. Needles are numbered to indicate size, from 14, the largest, to 26, the smallest. Keep on hand a variety of the usual sizes, 18 to 22, plus any special sizes that you use. A plastic pill bottle from the drugstore will hold an ample supply. Discard needles that become discolored or pitted.

To thread your needle, fold the end of a piece of yarn between your thumb and forefinger over the eye end of the needle. Pull the needle out of the fold and—still grasping the folded yarn firmly—push the eye of the needle down over the top of the fold. Pull the fold through, and your needle is threaded.

Alas, a good many people never can do this. For them a yarn threader is indispensable. It is made of metal and looks like this:

yarn threader

To use it, put one end of your needle threader through the eye of the needle, thread your yarn through that nice, big hole, and pull the yarn threader back through the eye of the needle. There. Your needle is threaded without loss of time or temper.

Choosing Your Stitches

In general, a relatively simple color scheme will allow you more variation in stitches than a more complicated one, which will restrict you to one or two. Many colors plus many textures make for a busy look that most of us find unattractive. In practice, you can do well with just a few stitches. From the front of the canvas three of these look just the same: the half-cross (for use only on penelope canvas), the continental, and the diagonal.

In the half-cross stitch, you work from left to right, and must turn your canvas at the end of each row.
Come up at the odd numbers, go down at the even numbers; turn your canvas at the end of the row and repeat. You may work it bottom to top as well as left to right.

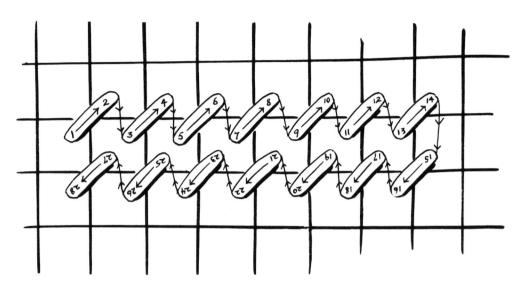

Half-Cross Stitch

The continental stitch is worked from right to left, and, again, you must turn the canvas at the end of each row. Just as for the half-cross stitch, come up in the odd-numbered holes and go down in the even-numbered ones. You may work it top to bottom as well as right to left.

Continental Stitch

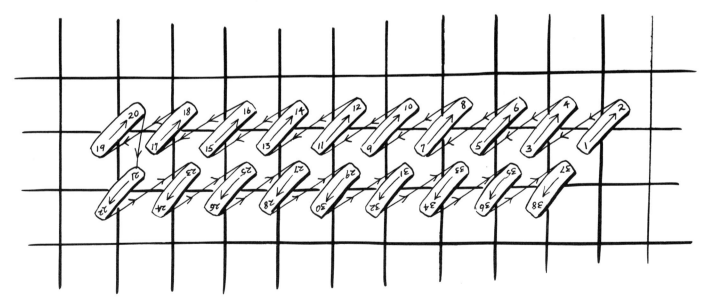

The Basics

The basket-weave stitch is called that because of the firm, woven look of the back of the work. It is good for backgrounds, and can even be worked on small areas once you are familiar with it.

You do not turn the canvas at all as you work, and you will see that on the rows going down the canvas the needle will point toward you as you come up, and on the rows going up the canvas the needle will point to your left as you come up. On the back it will look like this:

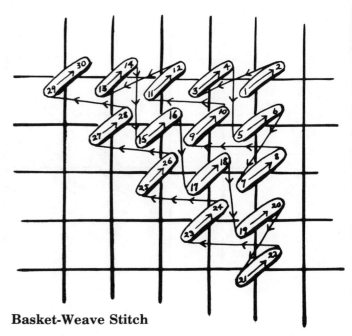

Basket-Weave Stitch

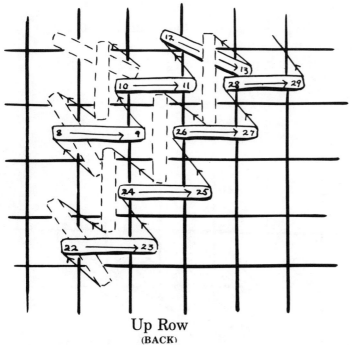

Up Row
(BACK)

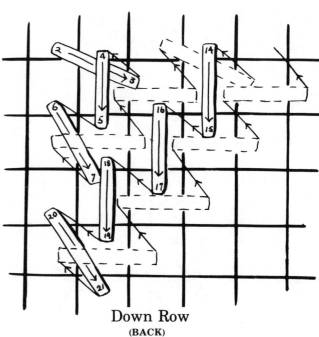

Down Row
(BACK)

Keep alternating up and down rows; do not make two down rows or two up rows by mistake when you're starting and finishing off, or a little ridge will show through on the right side of the canvas.

Another useful stitch is the brick stitch, which is a kind of small bargello, done over two threads.

Most other stitches are really variations of the continental, the diagonal, and the brick.

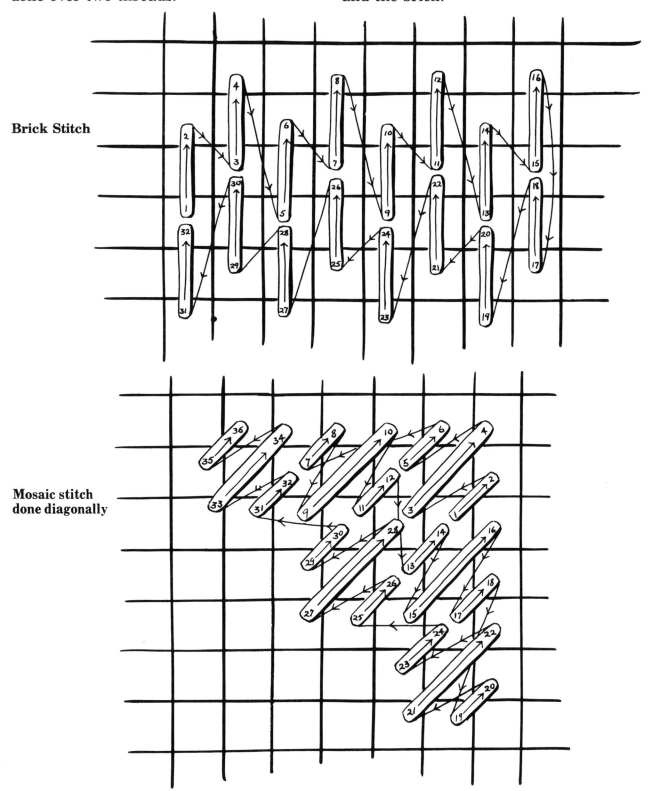

Brick Stitch

Mosaic stitch done diagonally

The Basics

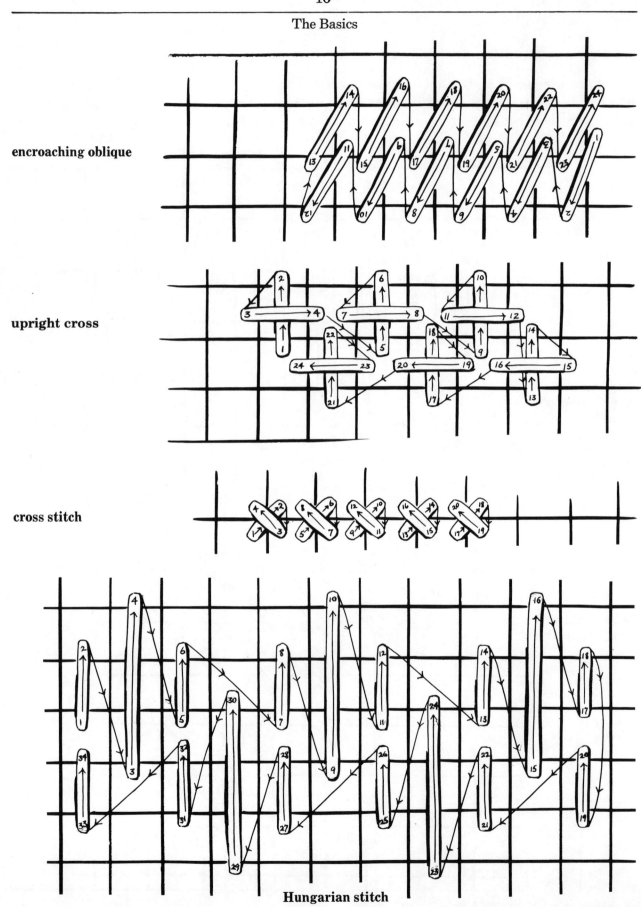

encroaching oblique

upright cross

cross stitch

Hungarian stitch

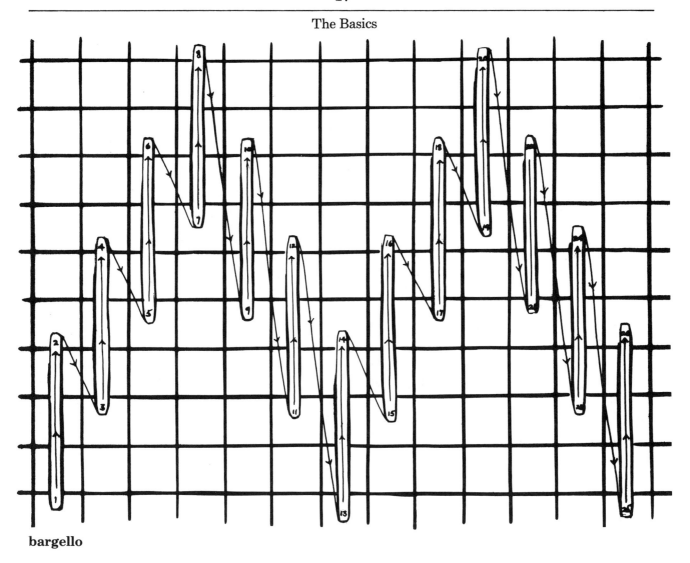

bargello

kalem

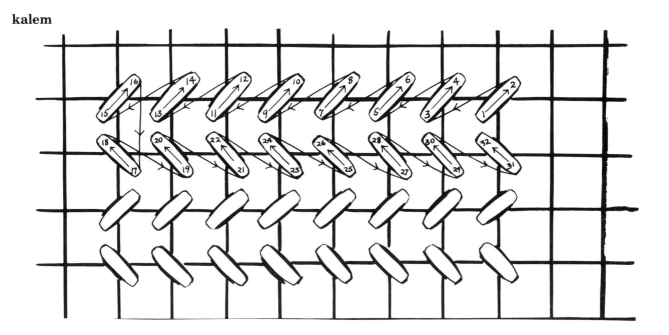

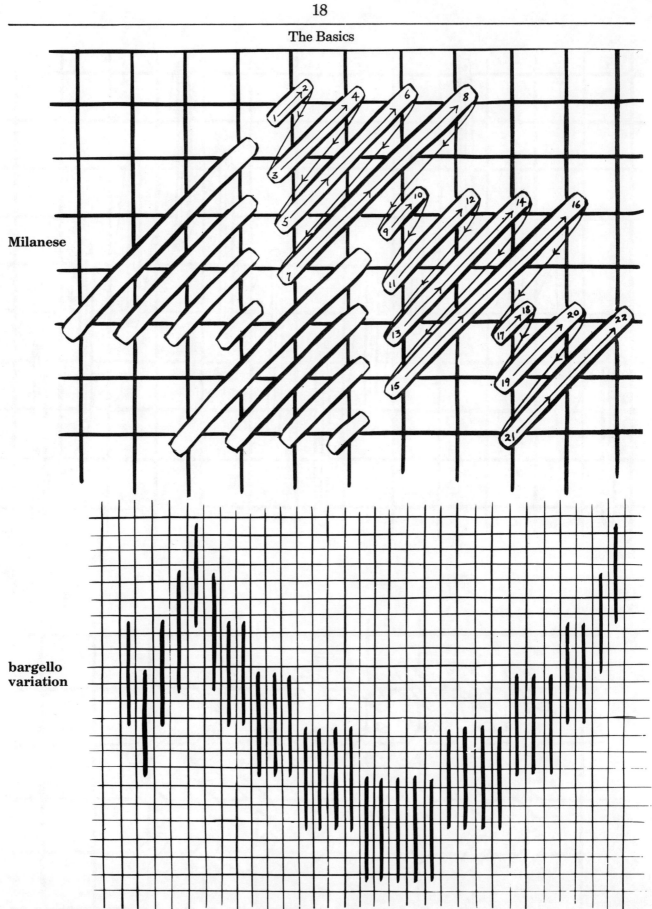

Milanese

**bargello
variation**

No matter what stitch you use, start your yarn the same way and end it off the same way.

To begin, thread your needle, tie a knot in the long end, push the needle down through a mesh of canvas that will be covered as you stitch this piece of yarn, then come up where you should to commence your stitching. As you stitch close to the knot and the end of yarn sticking up, pull the end taut and snip off the knot with your embroidery scissors.

To finish off, bring your needle and yarn to the back of the work as you complete a stitch. Run them under the stitching for about an inch—longer with loose stitching or bargello—and cut off close to the back of the work.

Various authorities on the subject propose different stitches for finishing the folded edge of a needlepoint canvas, which is a fine idea for many pieces. Most of these stitches have drawbacks, but one is perfectly satisfactory if you fit the wool to the canvas just right and maintain an even tension. A single strand of Persian fits 12 or 14 mesh monocanvas, a single thread doubled over fits 10 mesh; smaller-mesh canvas requires the use of crewel wool.

Trim the canvas so that 5 to 7 threads remain on each edge. Miter the corners as instructed (on page 32), working one thread out from the edge of the stitching; fold the edges just beyond that first thread so that the first thread out from the needlepoint lies precisely on top of the second thread out. Now run your yarn up from the back of the needlepoint, bring it up under both threads

right next to the stitchery, and follow this sequence:

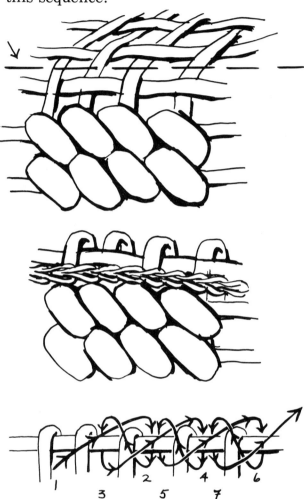

At first this is very confusing, but bear in mind that you are really making a kind of braid of cross stitch along the edge of the canvas. With practice, it goes very quickly. In this book we'll refer to it from now on as "binding stitch." You can use it on straight edges or 45-degree diagonals.

Stitchery is not really the subject of this book. There are numerous sources that deal with it far better than we could (see Bibliography), but for help with the stitches, the most practical guide we've found is the product called Stitch 'n Learn Needlepoint cards. Six sets of cards cover 24 stitches, with clear instructions right on each perforated and numbered card, and instructions for small projects using the stitches in each set. These are an excellent aid to teaching yourself or someone else a whole variety of stitches. They are available by mail as well as in shops.

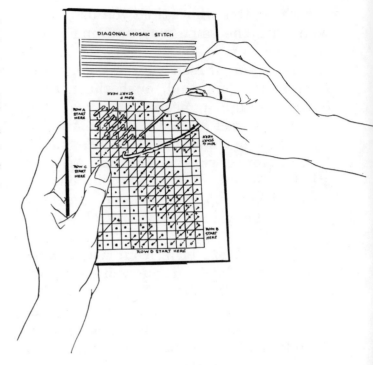

Frames

Most needlepoint can be held in the hand; one of its delights is that it's so portable. But if you are using stitches that will distort the canvas, incorporating silk or metallic yarns, or making something too large and heavy to hold with any degree of comfort, you'll need a frame. For a picture that will go in a square or rectangular frame, consider using one. The slightest degree of distortion in the canvas may become apparent if you don't.

Your choice of a frame will depend on what you're making. A bell pull, a bench seat, or anything else that would otherwise present an unwieldy amount or length of canvas can be put on a simple roller arrangement, available in three different lengths to suit standard sizes of work. You insert one edge of your prepared canvas into a slot that runs the length of a plastic roller, roll up the portion that you will not be working on, and tie it in place with a spare piece of yarn. Don't use the long pins that come with the device. The scroll helps to keep the canvas in shape, and keeps it clean and neat, since the canvas is rolled wrong side out and only a little bit of the working surface is exposed at a time. This is a great improvement over merely rolling the canvas around itself and tying it in place.

For small-to medium—size pieces

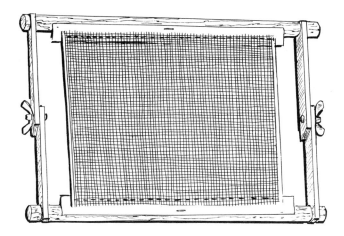

you use a square or rectangular roller frame, which comes with three pairs of horizontal bars in different lengths and a pair of adjustable side bars. The horizontal bars have webbing attached to them to which you sew the ends of your canvas. Then you roll up the excess on the horizontal bars, and fix the rollers to the side bars with the wing nuts provided for the purpose. You can also lace the sides of the canvas to the side bars for extra tautness. When you've finished a section, you loosen the rollers, wind the completed canvas onto one of them, and release fresh canvas from the other; then you tighten the rollers again and are ready to resume work.

You can work with the roller-and-bar combination by propping it against a table, or you can purchase supports for it. One of these is an arm that fastens to the side bar, grasping it

firmly but permitting the frame to be folded to one side for starting and finishing off. The stand has a flat piece of wood angled out from the bottom so that you can sit on it to hold the whole affair steady. You can also purchase a pair of floor stands that adjust to grasp the frame from both sides; a touch permits you to swivel the frame for starting and finishing off. About the maximum width that you can accommodate on the roller-and-bar arrangements is 22 inches.

For larger pieces, up to 36 inches wide, there are free-standing frames. The plainer sort are intended for rug-hooking but are entirely serviceable for needlework. More elaborate are the needlework frames that are truly handsome pieces of furniture which would not seem out of place in any room in the house. Some are made with wool baskets built into the supports. Both types of frame are built on the same roller-and-bar principle as the smaller frames. All of them are available in shops or by mail; we've described them in ascending order of cost.

Not especially intended for needlepoint but well suited to it are the canvas stretchers that you'll find in art supply stores. They come precut in various lengths and are easy to assemble. Tack the turned-under edges of your canvas directly to the outside edges of the assembled stretchers; canvas pliers will help you get the tension and perfect squareness that you want. The stands already mentioned for roller-and-bar frames will also hold stretchers.

Working with a frame has a different rhythm from working with hand-held canvas. Starting and finishing is no longer simply a matter of flipping over the piece of canvas in your lap. It seems awkward at first. For the continental or half-cross stitch, you either change sides or learn to work upside down. It takes getting accustomed to, but the results are worthwhile.

Naturally, you may prefer to use a frame only for the part of your work that really demands it. Once you've finished a design in continental stitch, for instance, you can remove the piece from the frame and fill in the background in basket-weave or brick stitch.

If you are simply concerned with relieving yourself of the weight of a rug or wall hanging, you have several other, less orthodox choices. You can drape your work over the back of a sofa, working from behind, or make some similar rig from an ironing board and a couple of chairs. It sounds peculiar, and perhaps it is, but it works.

The only sort of frame that you should never use is an embroidery hoop or any variation of it. Anything that must be pushed down over the canvas and tightened will make a mess of it rather than keep it neat and square.

2

BLOCKING AND SIZING

When you've finished your stitching—the whole area *minus* details that will be done in silk or metallic thread and *plus* a couple of rows on *any* side that will be seamed—you are almost ready for blocking. Clip the selvages every couple of inches and trim off any tag ends that show on the back.

You'll need a number of things for this process, so gather them together where you'll be doing the work. Essential are an ample supply of rustproof T-pins or wig pins, which you can find wherever macrame supplies are sold or in drugstores. Also necessary are a clear plastic draftsman's angle, available from art supply and draftsman's supply stores, and a board of some kind.

If you have a well-padded ironing board, it will work perfectly for small pieces or anything that does not need much pulling and tugging. Otherwise you'll need something more substantial. For years we used a sheet of plywood, drawing pins, and a hammer. Many smashed fingers later we discovered a leftover piece of the soft fiberboard Pat had used to make a bulletin board for her daughter. This material, sold by lumberyards, comes in a sheet 4 by 8 feet, which can be cut into smaller pieces with a light saw and little effort. It's cheap, soft enough that the pins slide into it easily, and firm enough so that they hold fast. It has one drawback—its absorbency. To eliminate that, and also its tendency to curl from repeated wettings and dryings, Pat keeps hers covered with a large sheet of oilcloth. All in all, it is great stuff,

Blocking and Sizing

eliminating the need for a hammer and preventing damaged fingers and bad language.

Once you have your materials together, lay your piece of needlework out flat. Is it perfectly square? Check it with your draftsman's angle to make sure. Is it only slightly out of shape? If so, you'll be able to pull it square with very little effort. Is it badly distorted? If so, it will need plenty of pulling to straighten.

Bargello pieces or pieces done mainly in diagonal stitch or worked on a frame are likely to be square or nearly so. There is little work needed on them beyond a light steaming with a steam iron, with the needlework placed between two terry-cloth towels. No sizing is necessary.

Mild distortion can be corrected by pinning the canvas into shape face down. Pin face up *only* if you've used raised stitches. such as French knot or turkey stitch. Stretch evenly and gently, and use enough pins so that you do *not* allow the lines of the threads to form reverse scallops. First pin one entire side in a straight line, then the first adjacent side, then the second adjacent side, and finally the bottom. No matter what the shape of the stitchery is, you'll be working with a rectangle of canvas at this point, placing the pins close together (no more than ¾ inch between them) along lines about an inch from the nearest stitching. As you work, you'll line up the threads just outside the stitchery so that they are perfectly straight and exactly at right angles to one another.

Once your pinning is complete, us-

ing a dampened pressing cloth and the lightest possible pressure on your iron, steam the stitchery little by little until it is slightly but evenly damp. The dampening will soften the sizing on the canvas, which will reset the threads when it dries again. When it is dry—and it will take overnight at least, away from sunlight or heat—leave the canvas in place and prepare to give it a light coat of sizing.

A piece that is more severely distorted must be handled differently. First of all, wet and wring out as dry as possible an old terry-cloth towel somewhat larger than the canvas you're working on. If you're working on a rug, you'll have to use a couple of sheets to accommodate it.

Lay the wet towel out flat, lay the needlework on top of it, and roll the two together like a jellyroll. Do not let any part of the needlework touch any other part, and leave it for only an hour or two—long enough to dampen the yarn and the canvas evenly but not long enough to have an effect on the dyes.

Then move the canvas to your blocking board, place it face down, and begin pinning one side in a straight line. Then, using your angle, a long metal or plastic T-square or ruler, and a pair of canvas pliers (all available from art supply stores) to help you pull, pin the adjacent side, the other adjacent side, and then the bottom. When you've finished, check the piece again for straight lines and right angles, let it dry, and prepare to apply a medium or heavy sizing, depending on how distorted it was.

These procedures will work for everything, up to and including rugs, but nothing will work permanently on a canvas that is distorted not just from the angle of the stitches but from too tight tension. Tension is as important in needlepoint as it is in knitting. Try to work as loosely as possible and still get the yarn to lie as it should on the canvas.

We can think of only two items for which you'd vary your procedure—round and oval rugs. These you stitch half an inch or so beyond what the finished size is to be, then dampen between sheets, and carefully center, right side up, on a piece of fiberboard cut to the exact dimensions of the finished rug. You pin the extra stitched area to the *edge* of the board, and line up the vertical and horizontal crosswise threads through the *center* of the piece to make sure they are straight and at right angles. When the rug is dry, the edge of the fiberboard will have made a smooth, symmetrical line on which the edges will be turned back. The rug is then turned over to be sized and pinned down every 2 inches or so around its circumference.

There are now available at least two easy-to-use blocking devices that eliminate board and pins, the Meyer Needlepoint Blocking Device and the "Blockit." The first will take a piece of up to 32 inches square; the second one, up to 22 inches square; and both are adjustable to accommodate anything from the dimensions of a coaster or a luggage strap up to the maximum size (see mail order section). Both operate on the same principle, and have four adjustable stretchers fitted with pins over which the canvas is slipped. The Meyer device, sturdier of the two, has cranks to facilitate adjustment and tautness, and a line of springs and hooks down one side to ease the difficulty of handling the last side. The choice between these two is mostly a matter of what size piece you'll need to accommodate, for both are simple to use and foolproof. An added advantage in their use is that since they hold the needlepoint clear of the surface on which they rest, drying time is shortened.

Sizing helps your canvas to keep the shape blocked into it. The cardinal rules here are to coat the back of the needlepoint evenly and never to allow the sizing to soak through to the front of the stitching.

The traditional material for this task is rabbit-skin glue—also used to size artist's canvas—available from art supply stores, and neither easy nor pleasant to use. It comes as a powder, which must be mixed with water (4 to 5 tablespoons of glue to a cup of water), allowed to soak and soften for an hour, and then heated—being stirred constantly to prevent scorching—until it is thick and smooth but not boiling. Then it must be set aside until it has cooled and assumed a jellylike consistency.

This gel is spread thinly on the back of the needlepoint with a spatula and allowed to dry completely. When dry it is clear, colorless, odorless, and very stiff. In theory, you can vary the thickness of the coating to vary the degree of stiffness; in practice, however, this is far from easy to do. Unless you have a canvas that is so badly out of shape that it really demands the rabbit-skin treatment, or unless you're making something that either should be or can be rigid, you can use something simpler.

Rice flour, which you can find in health-food stores, can be mixed into light, medium, or firm sizing. Use one part of rice flour to 7, 6, or 5 parts of water, stir the mixture until smooth, and then heat it, stirring constantly, to just below the boiling point. It will be clear and smooth. While the glue is still hot, spread it thinly on the back of the needlepoint with an ordinary paintbrush.

Both the mixtures will keep for about a week in the refrigerator, and should be returned to the proper temperature—cool for rabbit skin, hot for rice flour—if you are going to use them again. If this seems like a lot of trouble—and for small pieces it does—you might like to try an alternative. We've had good results with the ordinary craft glues, such as Sobo and Elmer's Glue-All, thinned and painted onto the back of the canvas, then left to dry. They are certainly easy to use, and they keep indefinitely.

3

HAND AND MACHINE FINISHING TECHNIQUES AND MATERIALS

NEEDLES AND THREADS

For finishing needlework you will need straight hand-sewing needles of the type with which you are familiar. Use what you are most comfortable with. You will also need curved needles, sold as mattress or upholsterer's or lampshade needles, usually in a packet with needles of several other specialized uses. These may be unfamiliar and awkward to use at first, but they are excellent for joining needlepoint inconspicuously; the curve allows them to pick up the threads of canvas easily where a straight needle could not. Practice makes perfect here. Remember that while you cannot unscramble an egg, you can take out the sewing on anything.

For machine sewing you'll use medium- to heavy-weight machine needles. Keep a good supply on hand. These are the regular sharp-pointed needles, available where sewing supplies are sold. Most good yard-goods shops also have special wedge-shaped machine needles for sewing leather; special supplies are available for sewing it by hand, but nothing in this book demands them.

If you want to use a matching thread, buy a heavy-duty cotton or one of the Dacron and cotton combinations. For rugs, of course, use button and carpet thread. For basting on anything, silk thread works very well and pulls out easily.

Invisible Thread: This is what you use for sewing on patterned needlepoint any time that it's impossible to match thread to the color you're sewing on. It's indispensable, though difficult to work with, since the transparent nylon filament relentlessly tries to reassume the contour that it had on its original spool and seems to have a life and will of its own. When you are not using your spool or bobbin wound with this thread, tape the free end so that it will not get away and behave like a wayward Slinky. You can purchase light-weight invisible thread at yard-goods stores, and the heavier weights where upholstery supplies are sold.

To use invisible thread in your machine, first wind the bobbin. Don't use the thread guide built into the bobbin-winding apparatus, but guide the thread onto it with your hand. Now adjust both the top and bottom tensions to their lowest settings, and test the stitching on scraps of heavy fabric; readjust until the stitch is evenly tensioned. This is pure guesswork—and infuriating—don't give up. Work with a slightly shorter stitch than you'd use on ordinary fabric.

When you are stitching, leave long ends. Reversing at the beginning or end of a line of stitching doesn't work well with invisible thread unless it is on a hidden seam. Pick up the end of thread on the front of the work with an ordinary sewing needle, bring it through to the back of the work, and knot the two ends together close to the fabric. Press with a warm iron to set both the stitches and the knot, then clip the ends short. Or, if your mood is adventurous, try what Pat does, which is carefully to

apply the end of a lighted cigarette to the ends a half inch or so from the fabric. This slightly unnerving procedure fuses the two into one and effectively prevents unraveling.

For hand sewing with invisible thread, use a double thread, and knot the ends. To start off, slip your needle between the two threads to catch the knot and keep it from pulling through. To finish off, take three or four tiny stitches, then do this:

Make a loop,

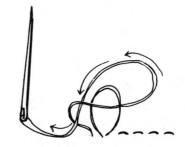

slip your needle back through the loop,

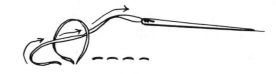

then go over the first loop, under the second.
Pull tight and cut the end.

This is also an excellent way to start and finish off any hand sewing.

HAND SEWING STITCHES

For working with needlepoint, whether you use a straight or a curved needle, regular or invisible thread, you'll need a small repertoire of hand-sewing stitches.

Running Basting: Simply weave your needle in and out of the two layers of fabric, making each stitch about ¼-inch long. Begin and end with a backstitch rather than a knot. Work from right to left.

Backstitching: Bring your needle up, then down ⅛ inch or so behind where you first came up, then up ⅛ inch or so in front of where you first came up, then down in the same hole where you first came up, then up about ⅛ inch ahead of that last stitch, and so forth. Work from right to left.

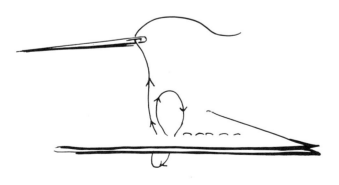

Catch-Stitching: This is the stitch you use to hold turned-under ends of needlepoint in place, to hold interfacings tin place, and so forth. Work from left to right. Start in the lower layer of fabric with a small stitch from (right to left), then move up and to the right and take another small stitch from right to left, then down and to the right and take a small stitch from right to left, and so on. The effect is a zigzag, and the stitch is taken so lightly that it does not show on the right side of the work.

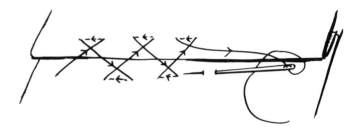

Slip-Stitching: This is an all-but-invisible joining, invaluable for many kinds of seams, for joining bias binding or ribbon to an edge, for attaching linings of fabric, and for joining two pieces of worked needlepoint inconspicuously.

For working with fabric, slide the needle through the folded edge, pick up a bit of the other piece of fabric, come back to your folded edge directly above where you came out, and repeat.

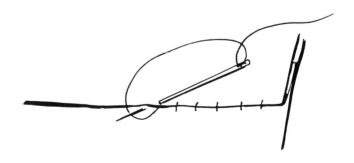

When you are joining two pieces of worked needlepoint canvas, this is done rather differently. You reinforce each piece with machine stitching, turn both pieces, pin them to your blocking board, and, with a curved needle and invisible thread, slipstitch them together just inside the first thread of exposed canvas, catching one or two cross-threads at a time.

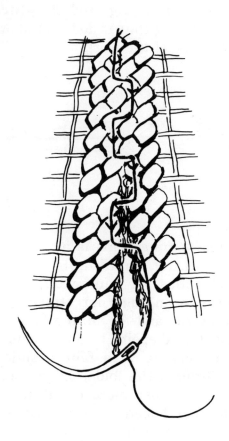

MACHINE STITCHING:

We assume that you either have your own sewing machine or have access to one that you are familiar with, and that you've done some sewing without having done a great deal. Armed with the manual for the machine—and a bit of familiarity with its use—you should be able to grapple with the sewing you need to finish your pieces of needlepoint.

Certainly needlepoint is easier to sew by machine, for, heavy as it is, it is very difficult to sew by hand. It is difficult even to pin; if you use pins to hold it in place for sewing or basting, you may be compelled to use the same T-pins you use for blocking, since regular straight pins will bend. What you can't pin you'll have to baste or paste.

When the instructions in this book say to reinforce trimmed canvas with lines of straight stitching, this means to trim your needlepoint canvas to about a half inch all around (narrower on small things such as watchbands, up to one or two inches on rugs), and then—stitching parallel edges in the same direction, to avoid distorting the canvas, and using the zipper foot on your machine—stitch two or three lines of small machine stitching as close to the needlepoint as you can.

Whatever you are stitching, sew with the grain, not against it; the grain is the direction of the weave, and sewing with it will keep you from raveling the threads of your canvas or fabric. On curved pieces, it is often not possible to do this all the time, but do the best you can. On rectangular pieces, sew parallel edges in the same direction. On a garment, a belt, or anything else with curves or slanted lines, your reinforcement will also serve as stay-stitching and will keep seam edges from stretching.

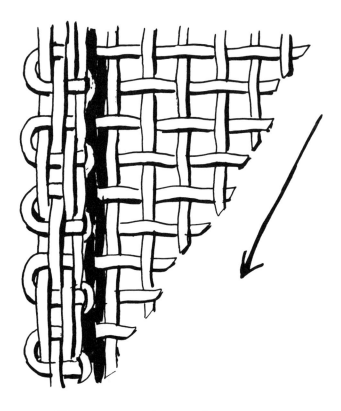

There are going to be a good many instructions for specific sewing techniques, so all that remains here is to ask you to familiarize yourself with the controls on your machine—the pressure on the pressure foot, the reverse, the stitch lengths and tensions, and the available stitches. Practice stitching on scraps of heavy fabric—lifting the foot with the needle in place to turn corners, sewing straight lines and curves, edge-stitching with the zipper foot about 1/16 inch from the edge of a folded piece of fabric, and so forth.

THE SEAM

To sew a good, clean-lined seam, you really must pin (across the stitching line)

or baste very firmly. Begin by stitching forward a half inch or so, then reverse, then stitch forward to the end of the seam, reverse for a half inch, and stitch all the way to the end. To turn corners, lift the foot, with the needle still in place in the fabric, turn the piece until the seam line and the needle are lined up, then bring the foot down again. For stitching curves, lighten the pressure on the foot and guide the fabric with your hands.

When your seams have been sewn, trim diagonal corners from the seam allowances.

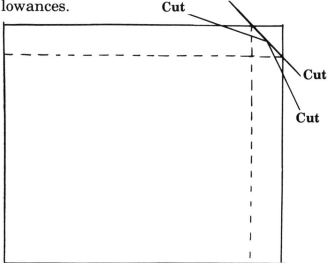

To reduce bulk, grade seam allowances to different widths, leaving the greater width for your canvas.

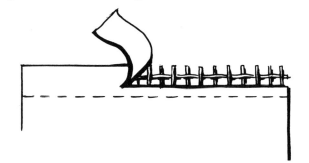

Notch and clip all curved seams so that they will lie flat. On a piece that is to have the canvas turned back before it is sewn—appliquéd, really—to a flat piece of fabric, notch and clip as you are turning the canvas. Obviously, you must be careful not to cut too far, but don't be reticent about notching and clipping at frequent intervals.

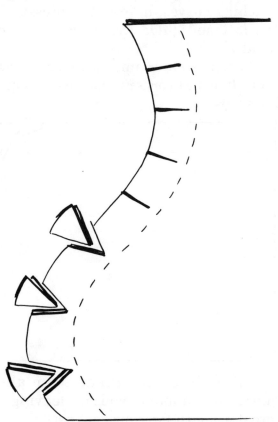

All seams hold best and lie flattest if they are carefully pressed flat after stitching and then pressed into place, flat to one side with the allowances together or opened carefully with the tip of the iron. Use light pressure and plenty of steam.

Mitering Corners: A related technique, designed to reduce bulk on corners of pieces that are to be appliqued to a backing, is the mitering of corners. On most such pieces you will have added two rows of continental stitching, skipping the last stitching in the corners, thus:

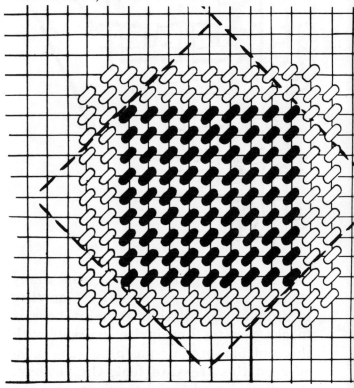

Then fold the corners back sharply, using your iron and plenty of steam. Keep the fold line on the straightest possible diagonal to the corner itself.

**Fold Line
for
Mitering**

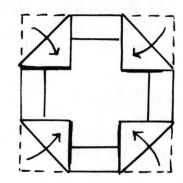

Sew or glue the turned corners into place (see "Adhesives," p. 35). When they are firmly set, turn the remaining canvas under, using your iron and steam to press excess canvas and stitching to the back. No raw canvas should show anywhere if you do this properly.

Glue can help in this process, but if you've blocked and sized your canvas properly, enough sizing should remain in it so that if you pin the excess canvas to your blocking board as you turn it, steam it into place, and then let it set, you can rely on it to stay put. Once you've done all this, the canvas should look something like this from the back:

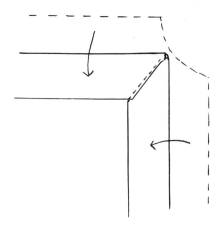

Those slanting lines are the miters of your mitered corners. Hand-sew them firmly into place; they have to stay put. Catch-stitch the rest of the excess can-

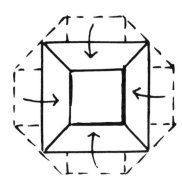

vas to the back of the work, and you are ready to pound.

There's an alternative, somewhat quicker method of mitering that you might like to try. Across your two added rows of continental stitching, mark the diagonal A-B on the back of the canvas. Then fold your fabric, right sides together, along the diagonal C-D. Using small stitches, sew firmly across on the marked like A-B; trim excess material, then turn your mitered corner to the back of the work. Turn back the remaining edges of canvas, slip-stitch them into place, and pound.

We've found, and maybe you will too, that canvas pliers can be a great aid in turning canvas and continental stitch to the back. They get a good, even grip on the material and hold it tightly while you press with your steam iron; they also keep your fingers out of the way of the steam.

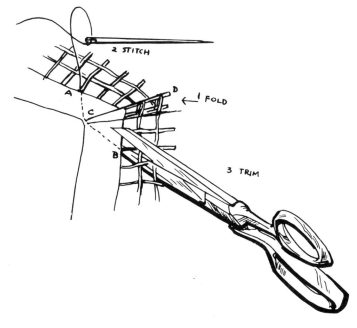

SPECIAL TECHNIQUES

Pounding: When you are given instructions to pound the edge of something,
the purpose is to achieve a good, flat,
sharp edge with as little bulk as possible. Pounding, with plenty of steam,
breaks down the springness of the fibers
in the canvas and yarn and allows them
to lie flat. Use a tailor's pounding block
or clapper or a hammer with a curved
(not flat) face. A cobbler's hammer is
best.

Sometimes, when the instructions
deal with preparing leather, we will also
ask you to pound it. Here the purpose is
similar but slightly different. The point
is to get the two pieces of leather—or
one piece of leather and one of needlepoint—firmly adhered to one another
and to break them down slightly so they
will act as a single piece. Pounding not
only does this but also prepares leather
to be sewed.

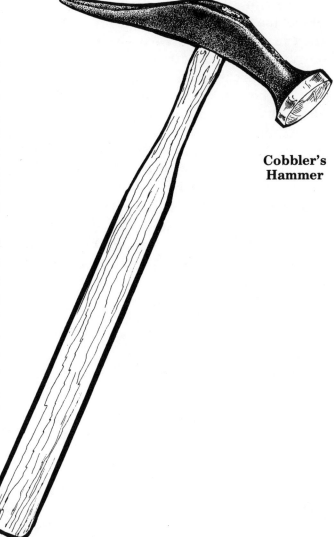

**Cobbler's
Hammer**

Pounding Block

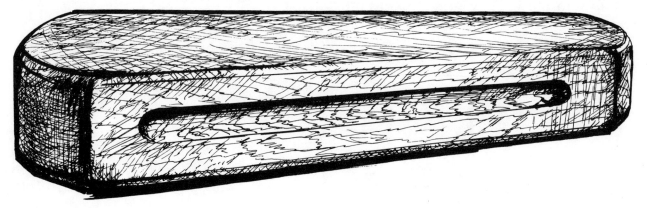

Hand and Machine Finishing Techniques and Materials

Adhesives: You have the choice of a variety of adhesives for working with needlepoint. Rabbit-skin glue, such as you use for sizing, is fine. So are Sobo and Velverette, craft glues from Slomon's Laboratories (a liquid and a creme respectively); Tri-Tex Rubber Glue and Tri-Tex Rubber Creme, and Elmer's Glue-All, from Bordens. For leather, use the special adhesive available from the Tandy Leather Company (see suppliers section); if you like, for a temporary hold, the other adhesives will be serviceable. Ordinary rubber cement is also good for a temporary hold. All of these adhesives are available at art supply stores and at handcraft and hobby shops. (See suppliers section.)

Clamping and Weighting: Quite often, in order to hold something in place temporarily, the directions will tell you to clamp it. For this, use large paper clips or clamps available from stationers and office supply stores.

When directions are given to apply pressure to something, do the following:

1. Roll the pieces to be adhered smoothly and evenly with a linoleum brayer, available from art supply stores, or with a rolling pin.

2. Put the pieces between sheets of waxed paper.

3. Weight them with a heavy book or put them between two pieces of board and secure tightly with C-clamps, available from hardware stores.

Making Eyelets, Securing Snap Fasteners, and Punching Holes: You must allow for eyelets and grommets when you lay out your pattern. Mark where they will go and omit stitching on those areas; do not carry yarn across the

C-Clamp

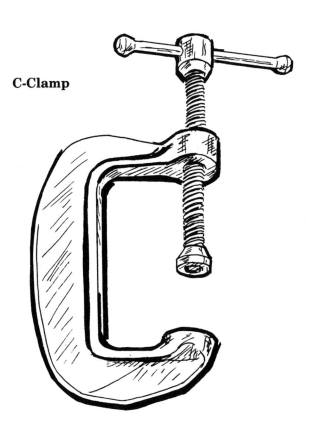

Clip

Clamp

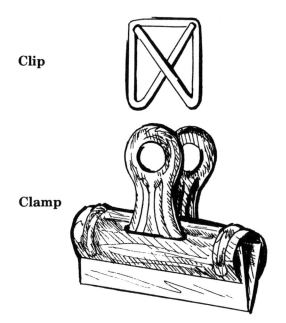

back behind them. Determine at the outset what size you'll need; an eyelet for a belt-buckle prong, for example, should be quite large so that the prong will move easily.

When you are ready to put in your eyelet, punch the hole through both canvas and lining with a drive punch and hammer or a rotating punch. Then place the eyelet with the setting tool, putting a scrap of nonwoven interfacing on the wrong side of the work, which will be toward you as you set the eyelet. Trim away the excess interfacing.

Use sew-on snaps for most applications. For a sturdier application on the flap of a scissors case, a garment, or something of the sort, use the decorative Western-type snaps, make allowance on your pattern to omit stitching, and insert a piece of nonwoven interfacing on the gripper side of the work as you set the snaps.

For punching holes in leather, use a drive punch and hammer. If you have trouble with this, an accommodating cobbler or saddler may do the work for you.

Cutting Leather: You can cut thin leather evenly and successfully with very sharp shears. However, the professional way to do it is to pin the piece out carefully on your blocking board so that it is taut but not stretched; scribe your pattern onto it with a stylus or ball-point pen; and cut it with a special leather-cutting knife or a mat knife with a fresh blade. Use a ruler and a French curve to keep your cutting lines true.

When you've finished, the cut edges of your piece may have a slightly shaggy appearance. If they do, light a candle and pass the edges alongside the flame—not enough to burn them, but just enough to burn away the bits of fiber that are sticking out.

If you want to try something out, use felt, which has many of the same working characteristics as leather, without the expense.

Cording and Binding: Many projects are enhanced by the use of some sort of cording, tubing, or binding. Pillows and cushions don't really look finished without one of these. To give yourself a good range of possibilities, you should know how to make and apply bias binding, cording, and tubing, and self-cording from spare yarn.

The simplest is cording from spare yarn. Take one or more lengths of yarn equivalent to about two and a half times the length of cording that you want. Put them together, clamp one end, and, grasping the other, twist the strands tightly for the whole of their length. Now grasp the twisted strands by the center, and allow them to wrap firmly around one another, stroking them between thumb and forefinger to even them out.

To keep the cord from unraveling you must stitch it firmly where the twisting loosens up near the free ends. Use a small stitch on your sewing machine, and sew through a piece of paper folded around the stitching line to keep the cord from catching in the machine. Remove the paper and fold the

The Meyer Needlepoint Blocking Device eases a tedious chore. The piece shown became, later on, the front of a tote bag.

Perforated card is an excellent medium for framed mottoes and bookmarks. It's shown here much enlarged.

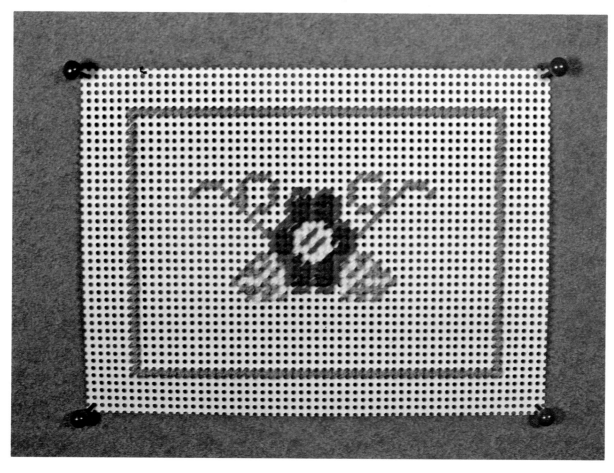

This handsome desk set, done with pre-finished pieces from Giftiques Unlimited, worked up quickly in masculine neutrals.

Sleek chrome custom framing gives a rich modern look to a chessboard and coasters.

Garden pinks and greens for an address book, also from Giftiques.

(below) Molly Feeley's drawing, traced onto canvas and worked in bold colors, became a permanent memento when custom framed.

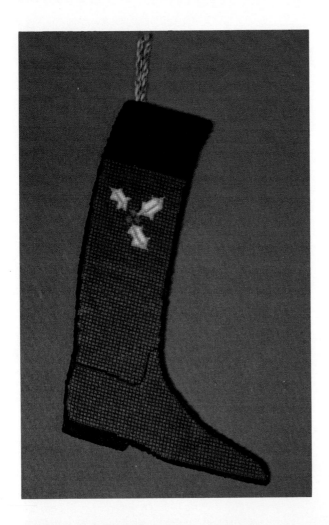

Merry but masculine, this Christmas stocking should please your favorite horseman. The background is a quick mosaic stitch.

(below) Beiges and blues the constants, stitches and patterns the variation for a handbag and purse accessories from Jacmore. The bag is an argyle worked in brick stitch, as a bargello variant. The eyeglass case is a brick stitch stripe, the checkbook cover continental on a mosaic background, the keycase a plaid done in a weaving technique.

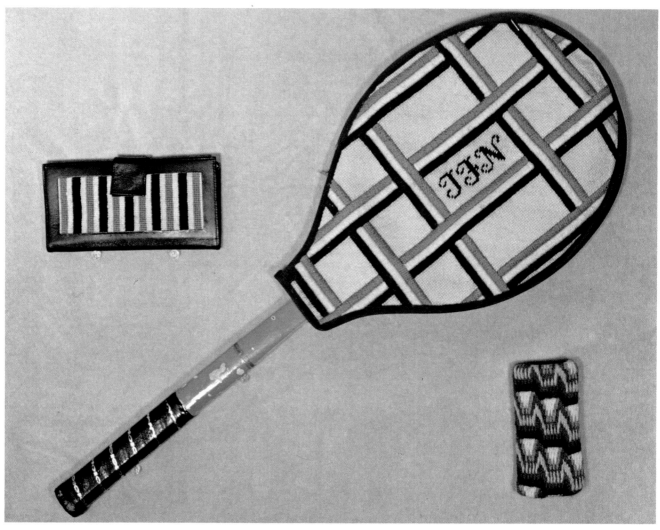

Blues and greens are the themes here. From left to right, a French purse by Jacmore in basketweave; a racquet jacket by Toni Totes a woven-ribbon bargello with basketweave background; and a bargello eyeglass case.

Set for a glamorous evening, this handsome bag from Jacmore was completed in black silk and metallic gold thread.

The Archers' brownstone, lovingly restored, is celebrated with this doorstop, in which the needlework is carefully fitted over a padded brick.

(below) A trio of pillows. A friend's favorite watering hole inspired the pillow on the left, adapted from a cocktail napkin. Center, bargello in a "baby blocks" pattern. Right, an octagonal pillow, a design adapted from a "Star of Bethlehem" quilt.

A lamp from Baxwood Crafters brightened by needlework adapted from a partially pre-worked doorstop; some border stitching was ripped out before the background was begun.

As practical as they are elegant, dining room chairs with covers worked in lattice-patterned bargello. They were started from the center block and worked outwards.

(above) To wear with jeans, this American Indian patterned belt was trimmed with bias binding and worked to fit a reproduction antique belt buckle featuring a Wells Fargo stagecoach.

Sunny colors against brown for a summer at the beach. The picnic basket sports a big luggage tag. The wallet is bargello. The monogrammed clogs are trimmed with bias binding; the clogs, from Tandy, were first sanded, stained, and varnished.

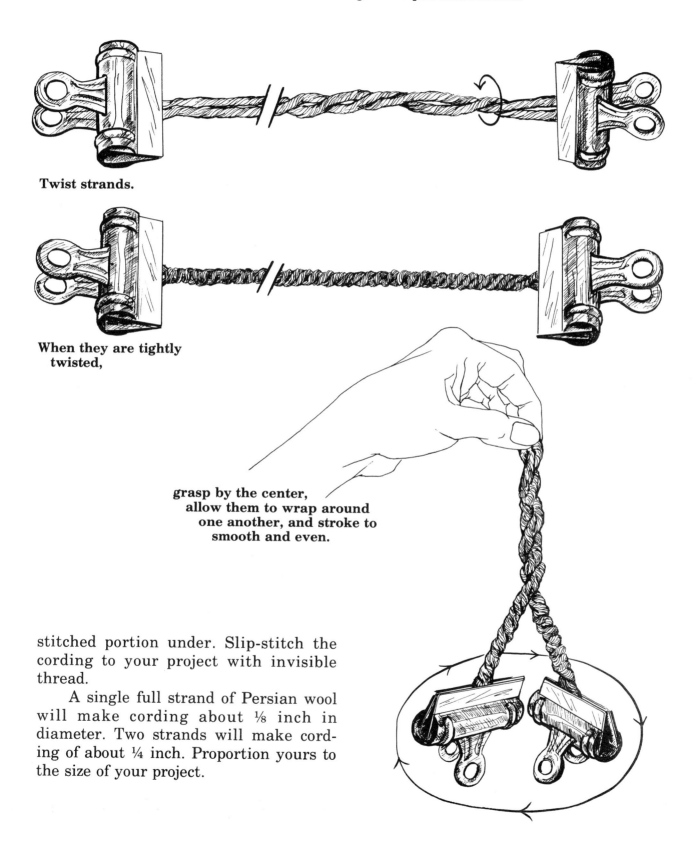

Twist strands.

When they are tightly twisted,

grasp by the center, allow them to wrap around one another, and stroke to smooth and even.

stitched portion under. Slip-stitch the cording to your project with invisible thread.

A single full strand of Persian wool will make cording about ⅛ inch in diameter. Two strands will make cording of about ¼ inch. Proportion yours to the size of your project.

Hand and Machine Finishing Techniques and Materials

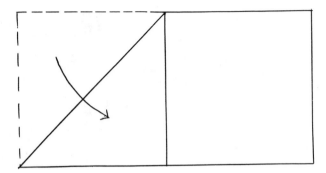

Length of Fabric and First fold

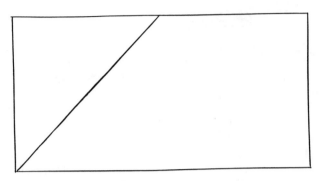

First Fold Marked

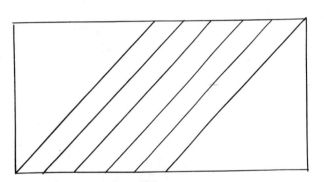

Other Cutting Lines Marked

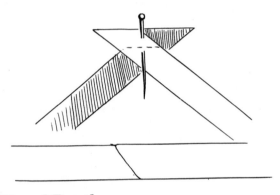

**Pinned Together
and Stitched**

Now for working with bias. Make bias strips by first folding the selvage even with the straight cut width of the fabric. Pin the fold, press it in, and mark it with chalk (tailor's or classroom) and a ruler. Then mark successive parallel lines on either side of it in the same way, using for a marker a straight piece of cardboard cut to the width you want. How wide is that? For bias binding, four times the width that you want to show when the edge is bound (1 inch for ¼-inch binding). For bias cording, enough to go around your piece of tubing—which comes in six dif-

ferent diameters, from ⅛ inch to 1 inch—*plus* 1¼ inches. For tubing, the same amount.

Now cut your strips out and sew the ends together, right sides facing. (Press the seams flat, then press them open.) Then, starting from one end of the strip, press it, stretching it gently as you do so. Now you have a complete bias strip, ready to use in one of three ways.

First and most useful is cording. Fold the bias strip right side out around your cording, and stitch close to the cording with the zipper foot on your sewing machine.

Hand and Machine Finishing Techniques and Materials

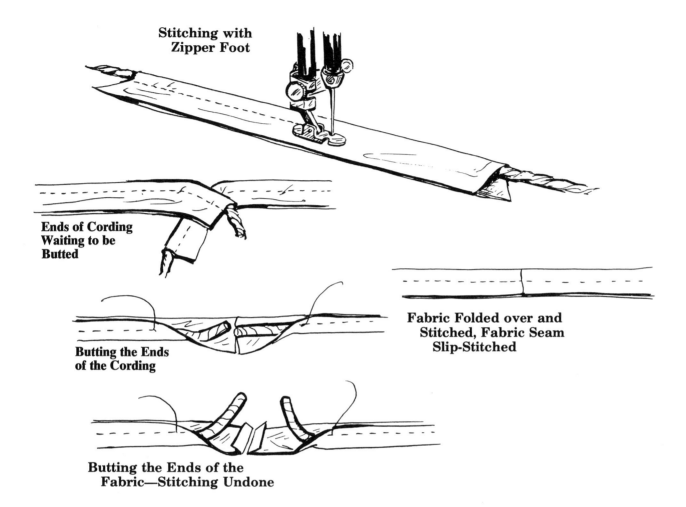

Stitching with Zipper Foot

Ends of Cording Waiting to be Butted

Butting the Ends of the Cording

Fabric Folded over and Stitched, Fabric Seam Slip-Stitched

Butting the Ends of the Fabric—Stitching Undone

To apply the cording, first baste it into place, leaving an inch or two free on each end. When you do this, you will be basting just inside the stitching line on the cording and just inside the rows of continental stitching that you have added to your needlework. The seam allowances of the cording and the needlework will be together, and the cording will fall facing in toward the center of the *right* side of the needlework. Clip and notch the seam allowance as you baste, so that it will lie flat and smooth against the needlework.

Now, using the zipper foot again, stitch the cording around, stopping short of the ends. Open the seam on the cording to expose the cording that fills it. Line up the two ends of fabric, fold one end back, and smooth the other over it; trim the ends if necessary, but do not sew them.

Bring the ends of the cord together, and cut them off so that they just meet. Fold the fabric back down, and stitch it into place. From the outside, slip-stitch the joining of the fabric with a curved needle and invisible thread.

Hand and Machine Finishing Techniques and Materials

To make tubing, fold your bias strip right side in, over a piece of cording. Stitch close to the cord with the zipper foot, just as you did before. This time, however, sew the fabric across the end of the cord firmly several times. Now hold the fabric in one hand and the free end of the cord in the other, and pull the cording back through the fabric; it will come right side out as a long tube stuffed with its own seam allowance. Snip off the end where the cord is sewn. You can make tubing firmer by increasing the width of the seam allowance, and softer by trimming some of the seam al-

lowance away. Apply it to your project with a curved needle and invisible thread.

To make bias binding, fold a strip of bias in half, right side out, and press. Then place the strip right side down, open it out, and fold each edge toward the center, pressing as you work. When you've done both sides, the edges should almost meet at the center of the piece. Now refold the binding along the center fold, and press the whole strip. You can preshape it to the curves of the piece you're applying it to by pressing and stretching it gently.

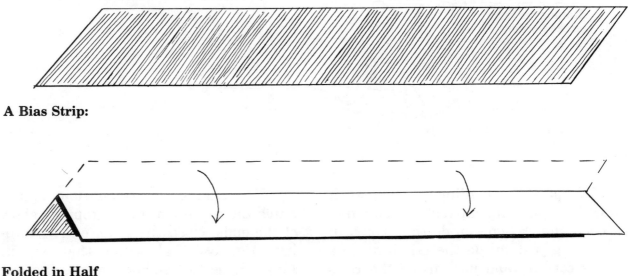

A Bias Strip:

Folded in Half

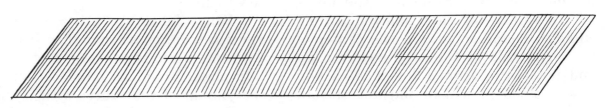

Opened out

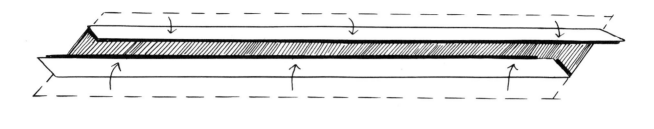

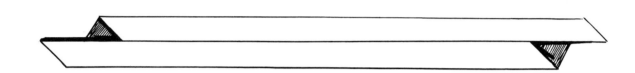

Both Sides Folded in

To apply bias binding to needlework, reinforce the very edge of the needlework with a row or two of straight stitching or zigzag where it will be covered by the binding. Trim the edge of the canvas even with the edge of the needlework. Unfold the strip of binding, and place one edge of the right side of the binding in line with the edge of the right side of the needlework. Pin, baste, and sew it into place, leaving the ends free, as you did for the cording; butt the ends of the bias strip just as you did with the cording. Then refold the binding so that the center fold lies on the edge of the needlework and the inner fold, next to the lining of the piece, is turned under with no raw edges showing. Press it carefully, pin the inside of the binding to the lining, and slip-stitch it into place.

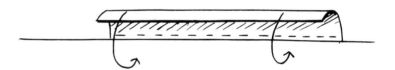

**Sewing the First Side of the
Bias Binding**

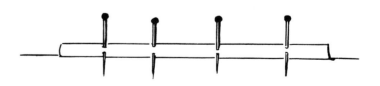

**Second Side of the Binding Pinned
into Place, Ready to Be Slip-Stitched**

Hand and Machine Finishing Techniques and Materials

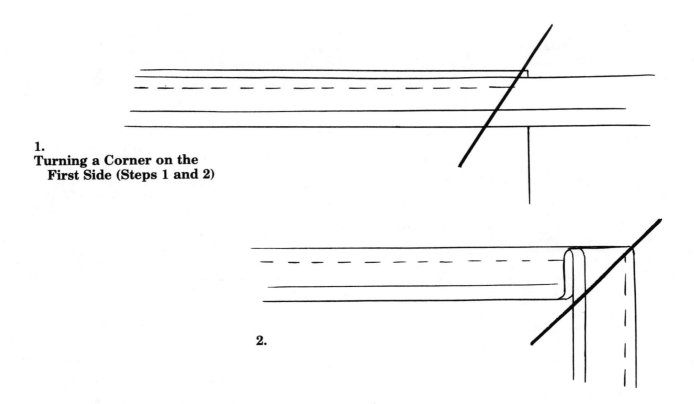

1.
**Turning a Corner on the
First Side (Steps 1 and 2)**

2.

Easy, isn't it? Well, yes, it is, on straight lines or curves, but corners are another matter. They are very tricky, indeed, but here is how to do them:

1. Stitch your binding to the line A-B and backstitch to secure.
2. Fold and press your bias strip along a diagonal line A-B, then flat at the corner and straight down the side.
3. To finish the other side, turn the bias over the seam and form a miter on the other side, with the fabric folded the opposite way to your first miter to eliminate bulk. Secure the miters themselves with slip-stitches, if you wish.

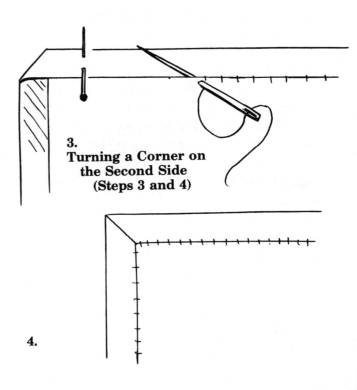

3.
**Turning a Corner on
the Second Side
(Steps 3 and 4)**

4.

INTERFACINGS, INTER-LININGS, AND BACKING FABRICS

Interfacings: These are what you use to maintain shape and firmness. They come in four weights:

Light, for reinforcing applications of grommets, eyelets, and snaps.

Medium, for maintaining shape in eyeglass and scissors cases and similar projects.

Heavy, to keep small clutch bags in shape.

Extra-heavy, for handbags and for objects such as luggage tags, which must keep a very firm shape.

The heavy and extra-heavy weights are made of woven hair canvas, the light and medium weights of a variety of materials. Purchase interfacing at a yard-goods store, and ask the advice of the person waiting on you, for there are numerous brands and types—some woven, some not, some iron-on, some not.

To apply an interfacing, cut it just a shade smaller than you want your finished piece of needlework to be. Catch-stitch it into place or adhere it with a fusing material, such as Stitch Witchery, *before* you turn the edges of your canvas or stitch your seam. If you are using a commercial pattern, use the interfacing pattern pieces that come with it, and follow the directions for assembling the garment.

Fabrics for Backings and Linings: A good fabric for backing should be firmly woven without being thick or stiff. Lightweight corduroy, velvet, velveteen,

suede, leather, cotton suede, denim, lightweight sailcloth, and medium-weight wools are excellent choices. Do not use felt, shaggy corduroy, or a print that would detract from your stitchery.

Lining fabrics should be fairly lightweight. Moiré, faille, light leathers, or light cotton suedes are good choices. For an eyeglass case you might want to use cotton flannel or chamois; chamois comes by the package at hardware and auto supply stores.

A good deal of the time in the instructions we've specified Ultrasuede, a nonwoven polyurethane fabric that can be washed, needs no seam finishing, comes in numerous lovely colors, and is the best possible choice for various applications. It is expensive, but a yard will finish a number of projects, and it's a delight to work with, having all the advantages of leather and of woven fabric, with the drawbacks of neither.

In a very few instances we've specified felt where it seems to us that the project will not be exposed to either moisture or heavy wear, neither of which felt will withstand.

In purchasing fabric, buy what you need, plus enough to making bias cording or binding if you are going to use it.

Sometimes you'll find it impossible to match a backing fabric to the colors in your needlework. The solution to this is to mark out on canvas the same outline as your needlework has, stitch in the appropriate color with a quick bargello stitch, and use this piece for a backing. You can make cording of spare wool and stitch it around with invisible thread.

4

PROJECTS

Flat-Finished Items, Large and Small

Anyone who does needlework is cursed with scraps of canvas that don't seem good for much, odds and ends of leftover wool in assorted colors, and a depressing reluctance to toss out these apparently useless leavings. And everyone, from time to time, would like to have a small but special gift for a friend or something small to be sold at a church or club bazaar. Fortunately, your scraps are perfect material for making small items—though if you're working from scratch, you should stick to making small things from fine-mesh canvas and larger things on coarser canvas.

Let's start with the luggage tag, a favorite of ours for a quick, small, personal gift. Pick the size and shape you want, work out a monogram and border on graph paper, select your colors, and do your stitchery, plus a row or two of continental stitch all round. Block and size. Cut a piece of heavy hair-canvas interfacing slightly smaller than the size you want your finished tag to be, and center it on the back of the needlework; catch-stitch it into place, or adhere it with a fusing material such as Stitch Witchery.

Now turn the excess canvas and continental stitching to the back of your needlepoint—mitering, notching, and clipping as necessary, and pounding out the excess bulk.

Cut a piece of light- to medium-weight leather or Ultrasuede slightly larger than the needlework. Apply craft glue or rubber cement to the inner surfaces of both needlework and backing, adhere them, and weight with a heavy book overnight. When the whole affair is firmly set, sew needlepoint and backing together with invisible thread, using the zipper foot on your machine and running the stitching close to the edge of the work. Trim the backing. Place an eyelet in one corner, thread the eyelet with a small chain or a piece of macrame cord or ribbon, and it's ready to grace a piece of luggage. If the bag goes astray, airline employees can differentiate it from others of its kind by the unusual tag; also, it makes the owner feel rather special.

You can make these with both front and back in needlepoint, use binding stitch for the edges, or vary them in many ways.

Variations

Key Rings: These are done in the same way as luggage tags, but they do give you a bit more scope in deciding on shape and design. Use either a chain or a split ring in the eyelet.

Coasters: Naturally, you'll omit the eyelet, and you'll finish the back with Ultrasuede or with the stick-on cork sold by the sheet in hardware stores.

Patches: A pair of jeans or a jean jacket can be decorated with a wonderfully bright and gay patch—monogrammed or just decorative, any shape or size. Simply turn these, omitting the interfacing and the backing. Sew them into place with invisible thread. If they

are to go on a pocket, you don't want to sew the pocket closed, so cut a piece of cardboard to slip into the pocket before you sew the patch in place. Use washable yarn if the patch is to go on washable fabric.

Game Boards: However large they are, backgammon and checker or chess boards are actually just like large coasters. If you will be using a game-board tray to hold your needlework, purchase it before you work out your design so that everything will fit perfectly. Skip the interfacing, use felt or Ultrasuede for the backing, and when you've finished, simply slip the work into the space provided in the tray.

Some trays come with a piece of cardboard slightly smaller than the opening; to use these, simply trim your needlepoint with slightly wider than usual seam allowances, reinforce the seam allowances, place your needlepoint face down, center the cardboard, and turn the allowances to the back of the board. Tape them in place with masking tape.

Tray Inserts: These work just like game boards.

Flat Christmas Ornaments: Do these as you would a coaster, without the eyelet. Back with felt, and thread at the top with invisible thread or a strand of bright yarn. If you wish to use a bit of padding or stuffing, insert before you complete your stitching and push it into place with the eraser end of a pencil. For designing your own, cookie cutters will help you with getting the proper outline.

Christmas Stockings: Make the

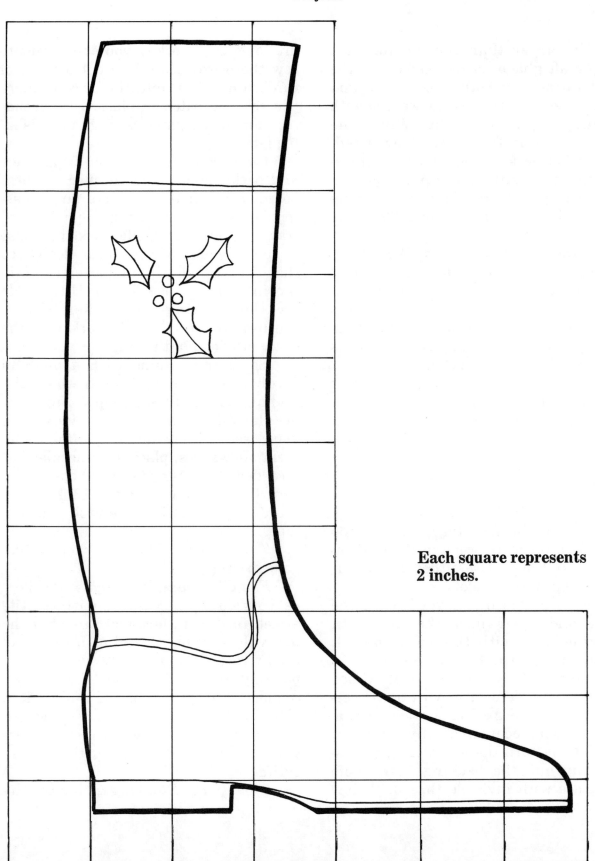

Each square represents
2 inches.

backing of felt, with a fabric-reinforced small cuff to turn under. To the cuff, on the inside, sew a piece of twisted cord made of spare wool or a piece or ribbon for a hanger. Machine-stitch the hanger before you sew the backing to the stocking; if you are using cord, a bit of masking tape will hold it in place while you sew and keep it from catching in the machine. The tape can easily be pulled away once the stitching is finished. Otherwise, the stocking is made like a Christmas ornament, though of course it is left open at the top; use binding stitch on the needlework at the top.

Inserts for Desk Accessories

There is a most attractive group of these available, including a box for pens, a desk blotter, address books, covers for telephone directories, boxes, and so forth. Each has an opening in the cover, and is furnished with a piece of cardboard that will fit behind the needlework and give it a sort of padded look; the piece of cardboard is imprinted with the size your needlework should be.

Trace the proper measurements out on your canvas, work your design, and complete your stitchery. Be very careful with blocking; to look right, your needlework must be absolutely square. When you have it that way, use a zigzag stitch on your sewing machine to stitch all around and just into the needlework. Trim away the excess canvas, down to the line of machine stitching.

Then lay the cardboard insert in place, and using the blunt blade of a butterknife or something similar, shove

the edges of the canvas down and out of sight, sides first, and then the top and bottom.

The nice point here is that you can, whenever you wish, change the needlepoint without damaging the objects. The supplier is Giftiques Unlimited (see mail-order section).

BELLPULL

Until we decided to write this book we'd never done a bellpull. We knew perfectly well that if we had one it would be used to summon "us", which happens often enough anyway. However, you might be luckier, or at least better off, and have some need for functioning pulls. Failing that, you might want a bell-less one just to cheer up a skinny bit of wall somewhere in your house or apartment.

You'll need needlework about 5 inches wide and 65 inches long, plus the hardware—a hanger for the top and a pull for the bottom. These come in several widths, so purchase the hardware early on and work your needlework to fit it. You'll also need about 4 yards of 1-inch velvet or grosgrain ribbon in a color to harmonize with your needlework, thread to match or invisible thread, plain cotton fabric for lining, and perhaps interfacing.

Complete your stitchery; do not add any continental stitch. Block, size, and reinforce. Before you trim, however, look at the thing with a critical eye. Does it look as if it's going to creep back into a distorted shape and hang catawampus on the wall? If it does, re-block and size it before you trim, and cut a length of heavy interfacing for it just in case. Cut your lining at the same time, and leave narrow seam allowances on both lining and interfacing.

Pin or baste your interfacing, if you need it, and your lining material to the back of the work. Sew all three layers together on your sewing machine, stitching just inside the needlework; it really doesn't matter whether you use matching or invisible thread. Trim off the excess interfacing, lining, and canvas right next to the needlework.

Now take your ribbon. Fold one end under and start at the top, applying it much as you might bias binding, but keeping it face up on the right side of the work. Pin it into place, using a single row of your needlework as a guide. Just as with bias binding, you go back later to slip-stitch the miters.

When you've got the ribbon neatly pinned, machine-stitch it into place next to its edge, using the edge for a guide. Turn the rest of the ribbon to the back of the work. Pin the long sides in place, and then slip-stitch them to the lining. Slip the hardware shanks in place and fold the ribbon over them, making a casing, then slip-stitch the ribbon to the lining.

This is a good-looking, neat, and rather simple way to do this. To remove the hardware for cleaning, you need undo only the slip-stitching at the ends (on the wrong side).

Applying Ribbon to a Bellpull

Stitch to edge of work. Fold ribbon on line A/B to the back of the work,

and fold again to the front of the work.

**Bellpull Hardware—
Hanger and Pull—
Showing Shanks**

WALL HANGINGS

A hanging, like a picture, should be blocked to perfect squareness or worked on a frame; otherwise, like a picture hanging crooked, it will annoy you every time you look at it. If you've had to block it into shape, make sure it stays that way; size heavily and adhere a firm interlining to the reverse. Use heavy tape, ribbon, or curtain rings to match your decorative rods, and sew them firmly into place with button and carpet thread. Otherwise, follow the instructions for the bellpull, which is merely a narrow hanging; however, between the lining and the reverse of the needlepoint, you may want to insert curtain weights to avoid any possible tendency for a curl to develop on the free-hanging bottom margin.

Your hanging will look roughly like this when you've finished:

PICTURES

Framing is beyond our capabilities and hence beyond the purview of this book, but we do have some tips about readying a piece of needlepoint for framing:

1. Because a framed piece will receive little or no wear, this is a good opportunity to use some of those attractive but shaggy stitches that you must avoid in things from which you expect durability.

2. Make an allowance for carrying your stitching about ¼ inch beyond what will show in the frame; the edge of the frame will conceal about that much of your stitchery, and it can be a disappointment if you haven't provided for it in advance.

3. Since a cardboard or fabric mat looks odd on needlepoint, you won't be using one, but you might want to stitch a needlepoint "mat" or deep border around your picture. If you aren't sure when you begin, allow enough canvas to decide later.

4. For a picture, your canvas must be perfectly square. Perfectly. Whether you block it into squareness or use a frame for working is your choice, of course, but please do keep this in mind.

5. When you take your piece to the framer, choose a simple frame that will allow the needlepoint to stand out, and that will not dominate it in either color or design. Allow the framer to trim the canvas to his own needs, and remember to specify that the piece be backed with a thin sheet of rubber foam; this gives the work a rich full look that can be achieved in no other way.

6. Don't limit yourself to simply framing a piece of needlepoint and letting it go at that. Below are some sketches of various framing techniques that you might like to consider.

a framed needlepoint picture

needlepoint as a frame, edged inside and out with narrow picture molding

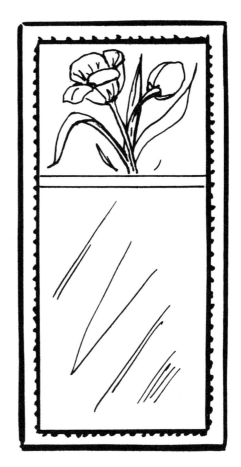

needlepoint above, mirror below for a handsome trumeau.

Director's Chairs

These aren't for outdoor use, but in an informal room, director's chairs with needlepoint covers can be enormously attractive. They are even less difficult to put together than a cushion or upholstery, since you deal only with pieces that are flat and easy to measure. Since measurements and construction of the chairs themselves differ slightly, you must use the old covers on your own chairs as a guide, and use these instructions to give you the method. Once you see what the dimensions are, you may decide to do the back in needlepoint with just a name or a title, and the seat in sturdy fabric. If you are daunted by the size of the project, you can try bargello, which works very well.

For most wooden chairs you'll need two pieces of needlework, a back strip about 6¾ inches high by about 27 inches wide, and a seat about 15½ inches deep by about 19 inches wide. Leave wide margins, at least 4 inches, on the seat. You'll also need heavy interfacing and cotton canvas or duck lining fabric for both pieces, two ¼-inch dowels 15 inches long, invisible thread, and thread to match your lining fabric.

Complete your stitchery, add two rows of continental stitching all around; block, size, reinforce, and trim, leaving ¾-inch seam allowances everywhere but on the sides of the seat, where you should leave 2½ inches. With these wide seam allowances on the seat, fold to the wrong side and press into place about a half inch of canvas, and sew it firmly in place with a zigzag stitch on your sewing machine. A half inch out from the needlework in these same seam allowances, fold again to the back, and press the fold down.

With all other seam allowances, do as you usually do. Miter corners, turn under all excess canvas and continental stitching, pound all creases flat, and notch at fold lines.

Cut your lining pieces the same size as your pieces of needlework plus seam allowances. Cut interfacing pieces to match. Pin or baste the interfacing and the lining pieces together, and then sew them with matching thread just outside the seam line. Trim the interfacing seam allowances away as close as possible to the stitching, and turn the lining seam allowances to the wrong side of the work.

Now place the interfacing pieces with the corresponding needlework pieces, wrong sides together. Taking the seat first, and using invisible thread, machine-stitch or slip-stitch the lining into place on the front and back edges, and machine-stitch it into place along the sides. As you sew it along the sides the stitching will form narrow pockets in the wide seam allowances at the sides. Into these slip the dowels. Then slide the dowels and the seat cover into the notches in the chair rails, and secure the seat by bringing up the arms.

Take the back pieces and slip-stitch

**Top Needlework,
6¾″ by 27″,
Fold Lines
Marked**

**Seat Needlework,
15½″ by 19″.
Leave
Ample Excess
Canvas on the
Sides**

or machine-stitch them together. Steam to set the fold line, and slip-stitch the ends of the needlework to the lining to make the narrow pockets that fit over the uprights to hold the back in place. Slip the back over the uprights, and lounge—as you deserve to do—in that handsome chair.

**Top, or back,
Folded for
Slipping into
Place**

**Bottom, or Seat,
Folded
Ready to
Be Slipped
into Place**

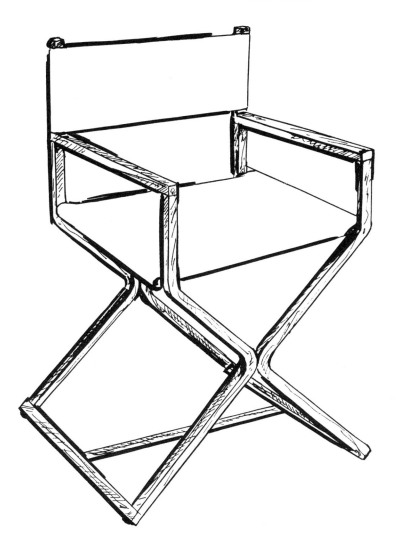

Belts and their Variations

Needlepoint belts make excellent gifts or additions to your own wardrobe. They are quick and fairly simple to do, except for the man's dress belt, which involves more work with leather than one is usually accustomed to.

We do want to emphasize a couple of things right off. One is that one's belt size and one's waist measurement are two different things; consequently, keep in mind belt size and the weight of the clothing over which the belt will be worn when you are planning length. The other point we want to make is to purchase your buckle while your project is still in the planning stage. A man's dress belt buckle is a simple thing to find, a standard item that comes in a variety of styles and widths; it will have little bearing on the dimensions of your needlepoint. But for most women's belts (or belts for men to wear with sports clothes or jeans in these unisex days), the type of buckle you buy will determine the length and width of the needlepoint. Also, of course, an unusual buckle can give you good ideas for a design for your needlework. Whatever buckle you purchase, make sure, *if* it has a center shank, that the shank is well offset behind the face of the buckle, so that you won't end up with an unsightly bulge in front.

Here are the backs of several different types of buckles. Most usual is the shank and prong or the prongless shank. Then come the shank and hook, with the shank hinged to the back of the

Buckles

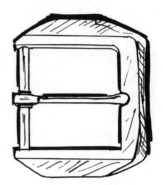

A. Shank and Prong

B. Shank and Hook

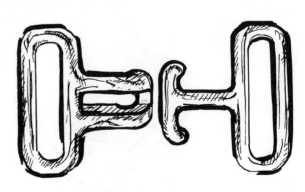

C. Interlock

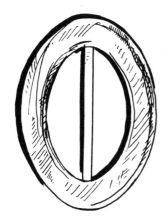

D. Shank

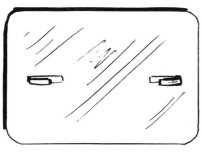

E. Double Hook

Illustration 2

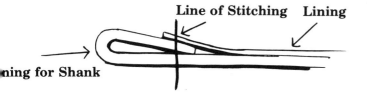

ning for Shank

**Needlework
Shank Foldover**

buckle; the double hook—grand, if you can find one, for use on a variety of belts; and the interlock closing with a shank on each side. The center-shank buckles dictate an overlap of several inches. The shank-and-hook and the double-hook buckles demand a length of needlework equivalent to the length of the belt desired *minus* the distance between the two fastenings. The same is true of the interlock closing.

In finishing all but the men's dress belt, however, you'll use just about the same procedure. Working on canvas of 12 mesh or smaller, mark out your length and width, with an allowance for an overlap if you need it and for foldovers at shank ends. Mark the canvas where eyelets will be placed. Complete your stitching, then add two rows of continental stitches all around, skipping the corner stitch at each corner. Block, size lightly, trim canvas, machine-stitch three or four rows on the canvas close to the edge of the needlework (use the zipper foot), and place the piece on your blocking board.

Use a steam iron first to miter the corners, then to turn back the excess canvas and the two rows of continental stitching all around, pinning the turnback into place as you work. Sew mitered corners firmly into place. Then, again using steam, go around the work once more, pounding with a pounding block or leather hammer to flatten the edges and eliminate bulk. On straight belts, notch the canvas every three or four inches so that the belt, when worn, will assume a smooth curve; on a contour belt, of course, you will notch and clip as you turn the excess canvas.

When the needlework is dry and firmly set, cut a strip of light leather or Ultrasuede a bit wider than your needlework but slightly shorter. This will be your lining. Coat the inside surfaces of both needlework and lining with craft glue or rubber cement, allow the adhesive to get tacky, then line up the pieces and put them together, curving them inward slightly as you do so.

Notch the seam allowance of the shank foldovers. If your buckle has a prong, make the eyelet for it. Position the shank foldovers with the shank or shanks in place, and clamp or baste the lining fabric over the end of the needlework, as in Illustration 2.

Again using your pounding block or hammer, pound the needlework and the lining together. When they are set—and you may wish to weight them between sheets of waxed paper with heavy books—sew them together, using the zipper foot on your sewing machine, invisible thread, and a medium-length stitch. Follow closely and evenly along the edge of the needlework; if you find this difficult, use guide tape to mark the stitching line. At the shank end, sew two layers of needlework and the lining together, as in Illustration 2; you may have to do this by hand. Trim the lining evenly all around. If you need eyelets, place them, and your belt is ready to wear.

For straight belts this is the procedure that gives the most finished look and the best durability. But there is a simpler procedure that works nearly as well. Skip doing the two rows of continental stitch. Fold over the edges and stitch with binding stitch. Treat the shank end as you did above, after hard pounding to flatten it.

MAN'S DRESS BELT

Using canvas no larger than 14 mesh, outline your design so that it is the width you want and 7 inches *shorter* than the desired belt measurement. Complete your stitching and add 2 rows of continental stitch all around. Block, size, trim, and reinforce as in the previous instructions, but this time reinforce the ends across the needlepoint itself and trim off the excess canvas evenly with ends of the stitching.

Turn, steam, pin, notch, and pound the long edges of your needlework, as in the previous instructions. Measure, cut, adhere, sew and trim the lining according to the previous directions, sewing it across the ends as well as along the length. This will give you a single piece of lined needlework to which you will sew the ends of the belt itself. Remember, if your design has a distinct top and bottom, the buckle will go on the left and the end with the holes on the right.

Now draw your patterns for the ends, using Illustration 3 as a guide. The wide part should be the same width as the needlepoint, the narrow part the same width as the shank of your belt buckle; the width of the needlepoint and the width of the buckle should be just about the same.

Tape your adaptations of the patterns to medium-weight leather, and impress them into the leather by tracing with a stylus or a ball-point pen. At the same time, mark the places indicated for holes and eyelets. Cut the leather pieces as indicated.

For the right end, punch or cut the hole for the prong, position the buckle, coat the inside surfaces with aehesive, let the adhesive get tacky, then fold the piece over. Pound together through the narrow portion, and place the two wide parts on either side of your needlepoint strip. Pound it into place, and, when it has adhered, sew it into place with

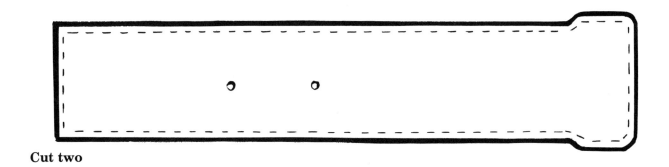

Cut two

MEN'S DRESS BELT—PATTERN FOR ENDS

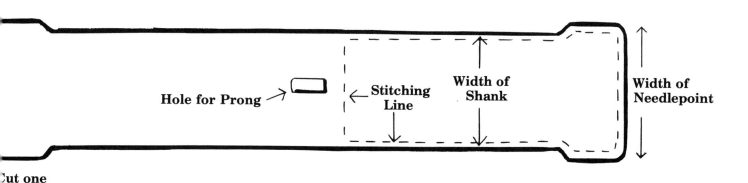

Cut one

Men's Dress Belt—Pattern for Ends

heavy-duty thread in a matching color.

Take the other two pieces, adhere them in the same fashion, and sew them into place as you did the piece for the buckle end. Now check the positioning of the holes, punch them into place, and the belt is ready to wear.

This is a demanding project, but if you can make it, you can make just about anything. Done professionally, the belt would cost about $50—so you should look on it as a real accomplishment.

Variations

Straps for a Luggage Rack: Do these exactly as you would a straight belt, but do not clip them, since they will not assume a curve, and treat both ends as if a shank were to go through them, folding the needlework under, then sewing the lining (grosgrain ribbon is good) in place, as in Illustration 2. Use upholsterer's tacks to fasten them to the luggage rack.

Guitar Straps: If you have a teenage son, one of these will be about the only needlepoint anything that he will use. Treat it as if it were a belt with two shank ends, and line with grograin ribbon.

Watchbands: Do these on very fine canvas, and use the smallest possible eyelets. Line with Ultrasuede. The buckles and eyelets for these are available from Tandy (see mail-order section). You can make them as you would a belt with a shank-and-prong buckle, or better, use the man's dress belt as your model.

Hairbands: Make as you would a luggage strap, but notch excess canvas so that the hairband will assume a smooth curve; sandwich a length of soft elastic between needlework and lining at each end, and sew into place. Line with ribbon.

Chokers: Make an inch or two shorter than the neck, put an eyelet in each end, slip a pretty piece of macrame cord or ribbon through the eyelets, and tie to fasten. Use very fine canvas. Line with ribbon.

Dog Collars: Make as you would a watchband, using discarded hardware from an old collar. Or make with a slight overlap and fasten with Velcro. Use 18 mesh canvas and a full strand of embroidery cotton, or you'll have to have it dry-cleaned.

Pillows

Here are some techniques for making pillows which seem to work very well, although some people may find them a bit unorthodox. These techniques differ from the usual methods in that the zipper is inserted in the center back of a pillow, or in the center of the boxing strip in the case of a box-edge pillow, rather than on the seam. It is rather tricky to insert a zipper in a seam that already has needlepoint canvas for bulk along with bias cording.

General Instructions
Decide on the dimensions you want. Measure your canvas. Purchase enough firm, medium-weight backing fabric for the back plus enough to make bias cording. Double the amount of fabric needed for bias cording if you are making a box-edge pillow and want cording on the top and bottom of the boxing strips. You will also need fabric for the boxing strips on a box pillow. Purchase a zipper, which should be two inches shorter than the seam into which it will be inserted in the case of a knife-edge pillow, and the same length as the finished length of the boxing strip into which it will be inserted in the case of a box-edge pillow. Buy matching thread.

You will need to purchase or make a pillow form that is at least one inch longer and one inch wider than the finished pillow itself, or one inch bigger all around in the case of a round pillow. This will insure that the finished product is fat and luxurious.

Mark your measurements on canvas and do your stitchery. Block the needlework according to the instructions in chapter 2.

KNIFE-EDGE PILLOW

Follow "General Instructions." Then make bias cording (see chapter 3) and baste it into place on the needlepoint, rounding the corners thus,

instead of squaring them this way.

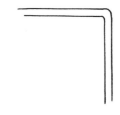

Follow instructions in chapter 3 for butting the ends and stitching the cording down. Now trim away excess canvas and cording seam allowances by grading the seams (trim each layer of seam allowance ⅛ inch shorter than the one in front of it). Now make the back. If your pillow is 12 inches by 12 inches, make two pieces each 6 inches by 12 inches

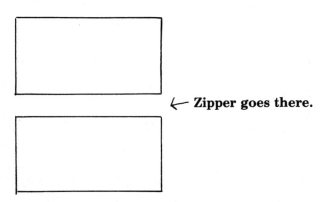

← **Zipper goes there.**

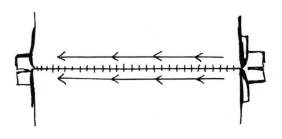

plus ½ inch seam allowance all around. Therefore the pieces you cut out for a 12-inch pillow would actually be 7 inches by 13 inches. The zipper will be inserted right down the center back of the pillow between these two pieces. Remember that the zipper should be 2 inches shorter than the finished piece (a 10-inch zipper is used for a 12-inch pillow).

Sew up the center seam first (it will be opened later with a seam ripper to reveal the installed zipper), using long machine stitches, and press it open. Now lay the zipper face down, baste and then sew it in place with the zipper foot of your sewing machine, top to bottom and

across, then across at the other end, and down from the top again.

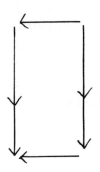

Open the seam over the zipper carefully with a seam ripper. Then put the backing and the needlework face to face, leaving the zipper open slightly, and sew like this:

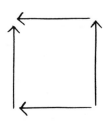

Grade seams, clip corners, and turn right side out. Insert pillow form.

BOX-EDGE PILLOW

We strongly urge you to make use of the fine commercial patterns available for box-edge pillows, especially the round ones. But if you are an experienced seamstress, you will find these instructions helpful. The method will work just as well for round shapes as for squares or rectangles or any odd shapes that you might dream up.

You will need to cut out three boxing strips for each pillow—one long one and two short ones. The two short ones are treated as one boxing strip when the zipper is inserted between them. Therefore one long boxing strip plus one short one equal the circumference of your pillow. Don't forget to add seam allowances all around each piece. The long strip should be cut to cover approximately three-quarters of the distance, with the short piece making up the rest. The seams joining these strips should be placed at the bottom of the pillow.

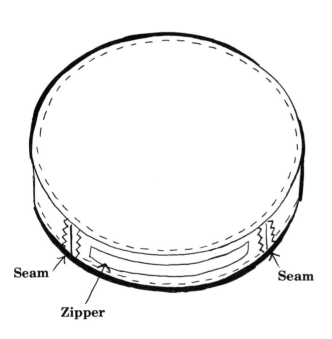

Wrong side

Fold the two short boxing strips in half and press, right side facing out. Baste the two folded edges together lightly like this,

using a catch-stitch. Baste zipper in place, then sew with zipper foot like this:

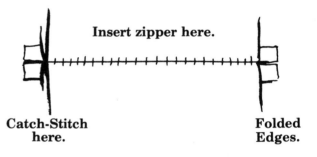

Open the seam over zipper carefully with a seam ripper. There's no need to sew ends; they will be secured in seams.

Make bias cording and baste it into place on needlework side, or to both sides if you want cording top and bottom. Follow instructions in sewing section (chapter 2) for butting the ends and stitching the cording down. Sew short boxing strip with zipper inserted to one edge of long boxing strip. Press seam open. Pin boxing strips to needlework and backing pieces. Begin by placing seam on boxing strips on one side of the pillow, and, right sides together, continue to pin until you work your way around to the opposite side of the pillow where the other boxing strip seam should fall. Sew that seam and press it open. Try to do that without completely unpinning what you have just done. Stitch boxing strip in place, making sure to stitch top and bottom in the same direction.

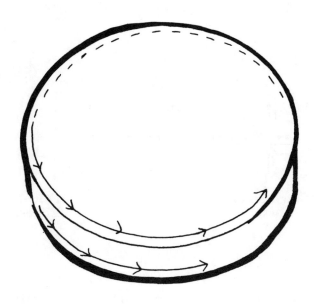

Grade seams top and bottom and trim corners if any. Be sure to clip seams on any rounded edges. Turn pillow right side out and insert pillow form.

PIANO-BENCH CUSHION

This is made on the same principle as the box-edge pillow, but without a zipper. (See section on pillows, page 59, "General Instructions," and page 60, "Box-Edge Pillow.")

You will need enough backing fabric for the bottom and box-edge pieces of the cushion and to make bias binding, foam rubber for the filling cut to your dimensions, about 4 yards of grosgrain ribbon, and a piece of finished needlepoint the size of your piano bench.

Cut velvet bottom to match needlepoint top, allowing seam allowances all around. Cut two pieces of equal length for boxing strip to correspond to the perimeter of the cushion, remembering to add seam allowances. Care must be taken when pressing velvet. Never press it with an iron. It must be steamed or pressed using a needle board made especially for this purpose.

Make bias binding following instructions in sewing section for butting ends and stitching cording down (pages 38 and 39). Sew one end of boxing strip closed. With right sides together, placing closed seam on one side of cushion, pin boxing strip pieces to needlepoint and bias binding. Sew second boxing strip seam closed when you have it properly placed on side opposite first boxing strip seam. Sew boxing strip in place. With right sides together, pin bottom velvet piece to boxing strip. Sew in same direction as top piece, leaving three-quarters of one long seam open. (It should be the seam that faces the piano.) Clip and grade seams. Turn work right side out. Insert foam rubber. Close seam, using an upholsterer's curved needle.

Cut grosgrain ribbon into four equal parts. Attach each piece by its center to the four bottom corners of the cushion. Tie ribbons around piano-bench legs to prevent the cushion from slipping.

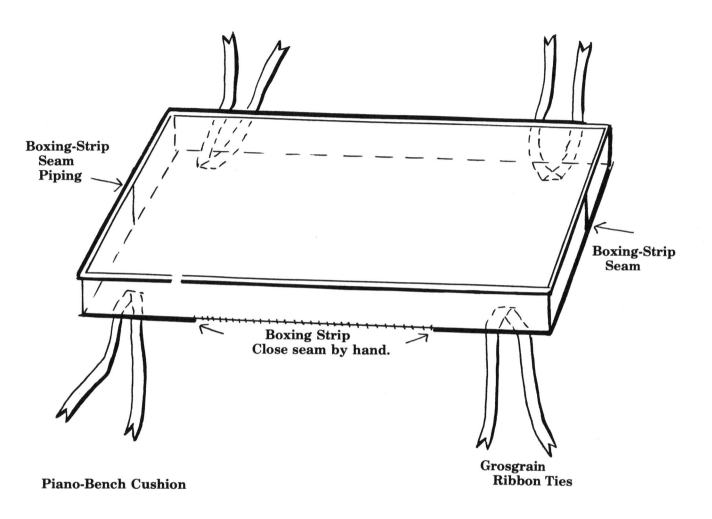

Boxing-Strip Seam Piping

Boxing-Strip Seam

Boxing Strip Close seam by hand.

Grosgrain Ribbon Ties

Piano-Bench Cushion

More Variations

STUFFED ANIMALS AND DOLLS

By all means make use of commercial patterns for these, although you most certainly can design your own easily. If you decide to design your own, here are some tips.

The best choice of design for these is a simple one, with a front and a back piece, and if you want the animal to stand up, a third piece for the bottom. You may choose to do only the front in needlepoint or both the front and back. If you use a fabric for the back, use a firm one.

To make the bottom for a piece, you will need either a piece of needlepoint or a firm fabric. Construct it as follows:

1. Measure the base of your project and double that figure. Using a tape measure, make a circle, and paper-clip one end of the tape measure to the measurement you need. For example, if the base of your project is 10 inches, you will double that and get 20 inches, and paper-clip the end of the tape measure to 20 inches on the tape measure.

2. Arrange the tape-measure circle into the shape of an oval, and when it takes on the shape that you want your bottom piece to have, trace it on a piece of paper. Add seam allowances, and that will be your pattern piece.

When doing a project with the front and back done in needlepoint, be sure to lay out both pieces on the same piece of canvas, 4 inches apart.

Design your project, complete needlework, and then block and size it. Sew all around just inside the stitching on your sewing machine. With right sides together, sew front to back, leaving bottom seam open. Trim, grade, and clip seams carefully. Stuff with polyester batting. If you don't have a bottom piece, simply whip-stitch the bottom closed using an upholsterer's curved needle. If you have a bottom piece, and it is made of fabric, attach it by whipstitching it in place with a curved upholsterer's needle. If it is made of needlepoint, attach it by leaving one

row all around it unstitched, then whipstitch it in place with yarn; of course, this works only when you are attaching it to another piece of needlepoint.

Variations

These projects need not be for children's use and enjoyment only. We have seen beautiful animal pillows of Staffordshire dogs and lovely dolls which look appropriate anywhere in the house.

These can also be made into doorstops. Simply fill them with cat litter instead of polyester batting. Do not use dried beans, because they might possibly attract crawly things.

PAJAMA BAG

We will use our turtle design to give you the basic techniques for this project. Make up your own designs, using children's books for inspiration or anything else that you think your child might like.

Only the top of this piece is made of needlepoint; the bottom is made of sturdy fabric. You will need a zipper, which will be inserted in the bottom piece.

Trace your design on canvas. The main body and all the other parts are traced and worked separately. Make the turtle as colorful as you like; you might also want to stitch the child's name down his middle. Work the pieces and block and size them. Stitch around all pieces on your sewing machine just in-

Projects

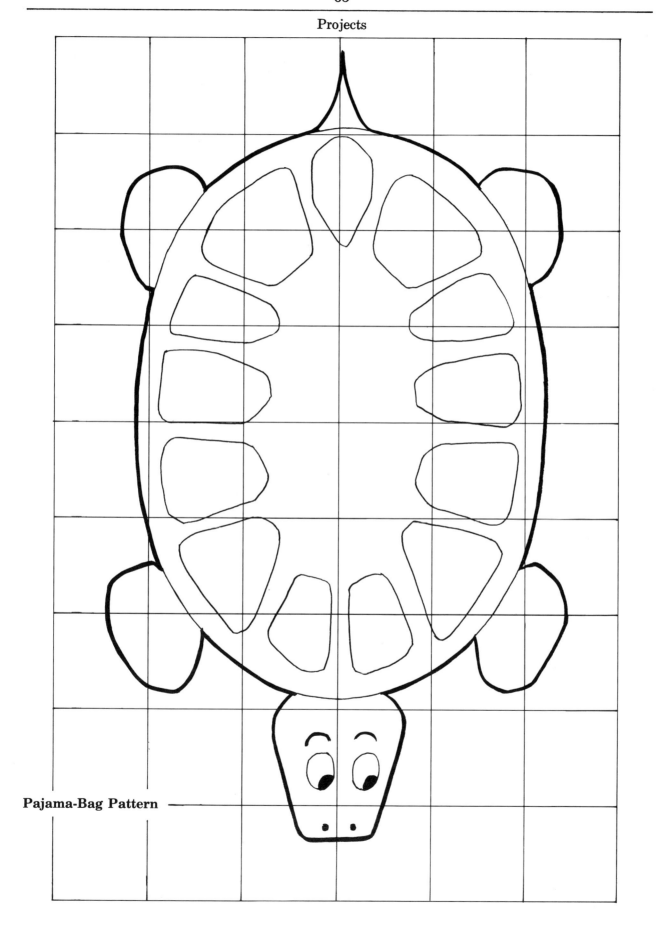

Pajama-Bag Pattern

side the stitching. The backing pieces are identical to the top pieces, but they are cut out of fabric. The one exception is the main body of the turtle. To make the pattern for the bottom of the main body piece, cut the pattern for the top of the main body in half and add about an inch to the center line on both sides, so that you will have fabric to turn under as seam allowance when you insert the zipper.

Insert the zipper in the bottom piece. (See instructions on knife-edge pillows (page 59) for zipper insertion.)

Attach all extra parts to their bottom pieces in the following manner. Right sides together, stitch all around, leaving seam open where it will be attached to the body. Trim, grade, and clip seams carefully. Turn inside out and stuff with polyester batting. Place feet, head, and tail on main needlepoint piece facing toward the center of turtle's back, with raw edges on seam. With right sides together and zipper open, stitch top to bottom. Turn right side out.

Cylinders

You can make needlework to fit any fairly simple shape, including a cylindrical one. In this way you can make handsome wastebaskets, lamps, and smaller objects. Naturally, it is a bit difficult to match up your design so that it meets perfectly at the joining, but if you're careful, you can do it. The trick lies in making a paper pattern right at the beginning. The example we'll use is a wastebasket. Variations follow.

Purchase an inexpensive metal wastebasket. It can be round or oval, with vertical sides or sides that slant outward slightly from bottom to top. Straight sides make the whole thing a bit easier, but you can work just as well with the others.

To make your pattern, take a sheet of newspaper. Place one of its cut sides against the seam of the wastebasket and tape it into place. Now wrap the paper around the basket, lap it over the seam, and tape it into place for a close fit. Trim the paper even with the top and bottom of the basket, using your shears; if the basket has rims that roll outward, cut just inside them.

Now remove the tape from the overlap on the side. Fold the overlap back until it is even with the cut edge of newspaper taped to the seamline. Crease it so that the edges of the paper just meet. Remove the paper from the basket and trim away the excess paper by cutting along the crease.

Fold the paper in half vertically and mark the fold. The line that you mark will be your grain line, and you should position the paper pattern on your canvas so that it will follow a single vertical thread of the canvas. You'll probably be rather startled at just how large the pattern is; we were the first time we tried it.

If you've selected a basket with vertical sides, your stitchery will be a perfect rectangle.

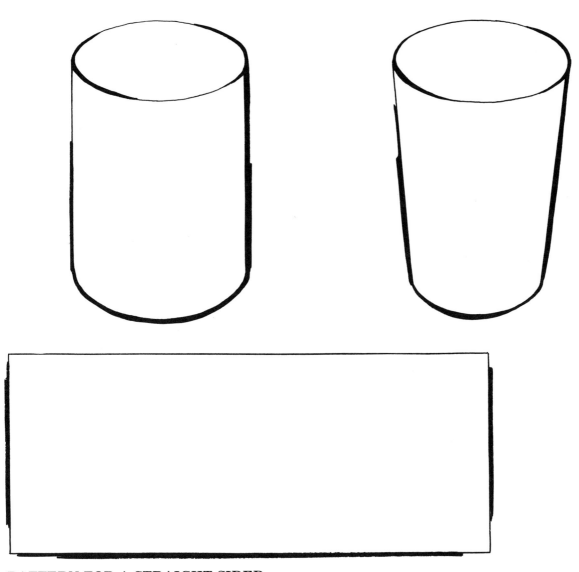

PATTERN FOR A STRAIGHT-SIDED WASTEBASKET

PATTERN FOR A WASTEBASKET WITH SLANTING SIDES

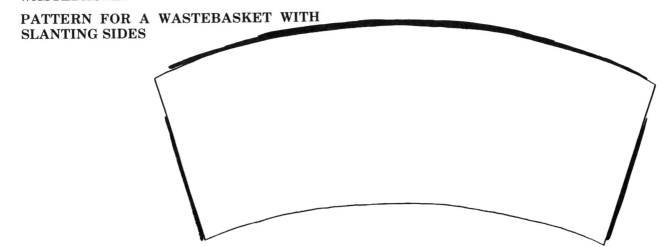

If you select a basket with slanted sides, it will be a fan shape.

Work out your design, complete your stitchery, check the fit of the piece by wrapping it around the basket, and fill it out anywhere that you need a bit of stitching. When you're sure it fits, add two rows of continental stitching top and bottom. Block, trim, and reinforce. On the top and bottom seam allowances. reinforce for the entire width of the seam allowances.

Miter the corners, and turn under all the seam allowances, plus the continental stitching on top and bottom. Notch and clip as necessary; a bit of extra notching, top and bottom—every two inches or so—will help the piece fall into a smooth curve. You can catch-stitch the top and bottom allowances into place, or glue and clamp them, after a bit of pounding.

Then, using a tailor's ham (if available) or a tightly rolled and tied bath towel (if not), preform the piece. To do this, roll the piece around your ham or towel, steam the whole thing thoroughly, and pound some more. It should assume the curve necessary to conform to the shape of the wastebasket.

Now put a couple of lengths of double-faced masking or carpet tape around the top and bottom of the wastebasket. Align one seam line of the needlework with the seam of the basket, and carefully wrap the rest around, adjusting it as you work and pressing it into place against the tape. The canvas should meet evenly at the seam line. Sew it up with a curved needle and invisible thread. Then steam and pat the seam into position.

To remove the work for cleaning, slip a spatula down between the needlework and the side of the basket to separate the tape, then ease the whole piece off.

Variations

Pencil Holder: Use for a base a clean soup can from which one end has been smoothly cut. Make your pattern so that the needlework will cover the can from just below the rim at the top all the way to the bottom, including the rim itself. Cut a circle of cardboard to fit the space left by the rim at the bottom and glue it in place.

Cover the top rim with a one-inch-wide strip of leather or Ultrasuede cut long enough to lap at the ends. Wrap the strip around the inside of the rim, tape it into position with any household tape, then fold it smoothly to the outside and tape the outside edge into position.

From the same material used for the rim, or from a bit of decorative paper, cut a circle slightly larger than the bottom of the can and a rectangle that will line the inside from the bottom to just below the rim, with the ends overlapping a half inch or so. Coat the inner surfaces of both can and lining with rubber cement, let it get tacky, and then smooth the lining into place.

Complete your needlework. Treat it just as you did the needlework for the wastebasket. For steaming and pounding you'll have to use a rolled washcloth or towel instead of a tailor's ham. Fit the needlework to the can, just as you did for the wastebasket, using double-faced masking tape. Cut a circle of felt to fit the bottom and slip-stitch it in place. Thus the bottom of the can will be filled out with cardboard and then covered; the can will not show at all, and no one will know from what a lowly object your handsome desk accessory was derived.

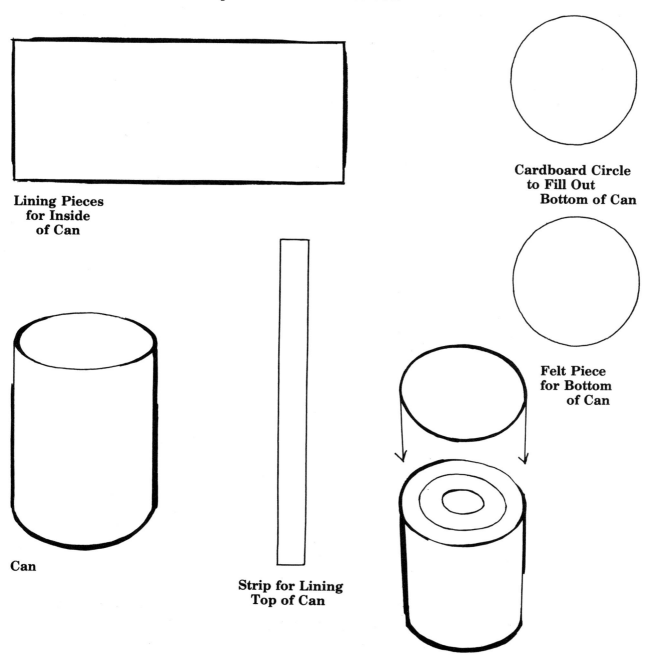

**Lining Pieces
for Inside
of Can**

**Cardboard Circle
to Fill Out
Bottom of Can**

**Felt Piece
for Bottom
of Can**

Can

**Strip for Lining
Top of Can**

Projects

Dice Cups for Backgammon: Make these just as you would a pencil holder, using small size tomato-paste or frozen-orange-juice cans.

Small Dishes for Paper Clips: The same. Use a tuna or cat-food can.

Inserts for Lucite Ice Buckets, Lamps, or Wastebaskets: These work out best if you use a firm interfacing in them. And since you absolutely must not go near Lucite with an iron in your hand, you'll have to do your seaming, preforming, and fitting on your ham, with frequent checks to see how the fitting is coming along. For the ice bucket or wastebasket, use felt, slip-stitched into place, for a lining.

Lamp with a Wooden Base: Purch-

ase a finished or unfinished lamp base with a straight-sided, cylindrical center column, something like this.

Finish the base in a color to harmonize with your needlework. Proceed as for the wastebasket. Your pressing will work out best if you do it over a seam roll; if you don't have one, a rolling pin covered with several thicknesses of toweling will do. Slip-stitch into place after securing with double-faced masking or carpet tape.

Napkin Rings: These are annoying because of their small size—5 to 6 inches long, 1 to 1½ inches wide. The best method I've found for them is to cut the canvas about 3 inches longer and ¾ inch wider than the dimensions of your ring,

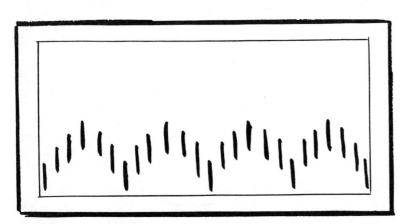

**Needlework Plus
Seam Allowances**

LAMP WITH WOODEN BASE AND NEEDLEPOINT INSERT

and to fold under and press the canvas on the long sides, matching it mesh for mesh so that it will be easy to bind with binding stitch later. Press it with a steam iron; the sizing in the canvas will adhere it in place almost as well as glue.

Do your stitchery, working over the threads at the sides as if they were one layer of canvas. When you've completed your stitchery, block, pinning only on the ends. Trim and reinforce the ends of the canvas and turn them under. Seam with curved needle and invisible thread.

Work binding stitch all around the top and bottom edges of the canvas.

Cut a piece of grosgrain ribbon slightly longer and the same width as your finished needlework. This will be your lining. Slip it inside the ring, butt the ends, and crease them with your fingers to mark where the seam will go. Seam the ribbon, using a straight stitch on your sewing machine. Press the seam flat, then press it open. Slip the circle of ribbon into the ring, wrong sides together, and slip-stitch it in place.

Box Shapes

A brick cover for a doorstop or bookend is usually the first box-shaped piece that one is apt to try. They are usually done on 14 mesh canvas—though 10 mesh will do—and because they are fairly small, they are quick to do. Most covers are made for a brick 2½ × 8½ × 4½ inches that will lie with its wide side down, but you can make them to stand on end or on a narrow side. You can also add shaping with styrofoam; cut it with a serrated frozen-food knife, shape it with a heavy file or rasp, and glue it into place with a heavy coating of craft glue on both styrofoam and brick. By turning your brick different ways and adding shaping, you can work out designs that resemble houses or barns, trucks or buses, railway engines or racing cars.

Most bricks should be washed before you work with them. A brush and detergent or a cycle in the dishwasher will get rid of dust and dirt. Once the brick is dry, apply what shaping you want, measure carefully, and mark out your pattern on canvas.

When you've completed your stitching, add two rows of continental stitch to the outside edges only, not to the seam lines. Block, size, reinforce, and trim your canvas, leaving an inch or so on the outside seam lines.

Now, using several layers of soft cotton flannel, make a jacket for your brick. While your needlework pattern had five faces (four sides and the top), there being no stitchery for the bottom, this jacket will have six. Don't forget to leave seam allowances.

Wrap the jacket around the brick and catch-stitch it together. Then pin the needlework to the flannel while you slip-stitch the seam lines together with a curved needle and invisible thread. Turn under the remaining canvas, miter the corners, and catch-stitch the canvas edges to the flannel. Press flat, cut a piece of felt to the dimensions of the bottom, and slip-stitch the felt into place.

Variations

Tissue Boxes: Use a basswood box, found in needlecraft or hobby shops (see also mail-order section), and measure carefully to make your pattern. It will have five sides, with an opening in the center:

Work out your design; four-way bargello is particularly effective on these. Complete your stitching. Add two rows of continental stitching to the edges of the opening and to the free sides, but not to the seam lines. Block, size, reinforce, and trim. Turn back the edges around the opening first, clipping as you go, and catch-stitch them in place.

Sand the box lightly to smooth out rough edges. You need not pad it, though you may do so if you want a soft, rounded look.

Pin the needlework in place on top of the box while you slip-stitch the seam lines with a curved needle and invisible thread. Carry the seam line nearly to the edge of the raw canvas. Slip the

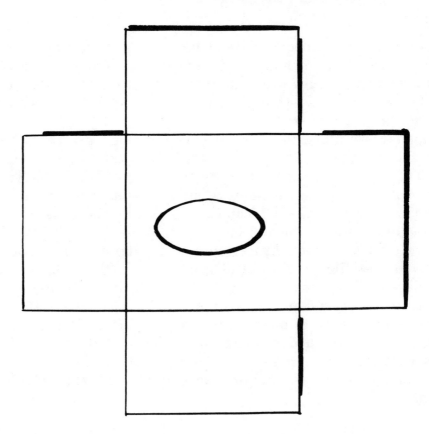

needlepoint gently from the box. Notch the seam allowance at each corner where it will be turned under; press the allowance above the notch to one side, and the allowance below the notch to the other side.

Now, working with a steam iron and pins, one side at a time, turn under the excess canvas and continental stitching. Pound. Glue the turn-under to the back of the needlework and clamp in place until dry.

When the edges on all four sides are turned under and firmly set, lightly coat the entire outside of the box and the entire inside of the needlework with craft glue. When the glue is tacky, fit the needlework over the box; as you work, wipe away the excess glue with a damp rag or sponge. Clamp along the edges until the glue sets.

If you wish, glue a length of grosgrain or velvet ribbon a quarter-inch wide around the inside of the opening.

Boxes with Hinged Lids: We don't think these come off very well, because the bulk of the needlework makes it difficult to achieve smooth, sharp lines, but if you use canvas 14 mesh or smaller, you can probably manage to get a neat finish. Purchase your box, measure carefully, and draw two pattern pieces; the piece for the lower half of the box will have no stitching on the center portion, which will be the bottom of the box.

Complete your stitching. Add continental stitching as before, block, reinforce, and trim. Proceed as with the tissue box, placing each half in turn on the proper section of the box. When both

sections are complete, slip-stitch a piece of felt to the bottom of the box.

Put the top and bottom of the box together, and tie them as you would a package.

This will keep the two pieces in alignment while you fasten the hardware. Use purchased hardware from a hobby or handcraft shop or from the hardware store—anything that is well proportioned to the size of the box—and screw the hinges and catch in place right through the needlework and into the wood.

If you wish to line your box, cut attractive wrapping paper or one of the handsome handmade book papers to fit, coat the inside of the box and the back of the paper with a light coat of rubber cement, and smooth the lining in place.

Covers and Cases for All Kinds of Things

Around Pat's house the object that used to be most often misplaced was the *TV Guide*—usually just at the moment when the children were watching something she objected to and when she knew that there was something like a good wildlife show on some other channel. So she made a small jacket for the magazine, to make it more readily visible. The method is similar to that for the jewelry roll that comes later on in the book, and this—or one of its variations—is good practice for that more complicated job.

To make it, you'll need a piece of needlework 8⅜ inches high by 11¼ inches wide; it will fold down the center, so work out a design that will accommodate itself to the fold. You'll also need leather adhesive or rubber cement, invisible thread and thread to match your lining material, leather needles for your sewing machine, leather or Ultrasuede lining material cut to the same measurements as the needlework, two strips of the lining material 9⅜ inches by 1¼ inches, and two interfacing strips 9⅜ inches by ½ inch. The strips will hold your *TV Guide* in place.

Complete your stitchery. Add two rows of continental stitching all around. Block, trim, and reinforce. Miter corners, and turn excess canvas and continental stitching to the wrong side of the piece. Pound. Catch-stitch or adhere the seam allowances in place. Set aside.

Center and adhere the interfacing strips to the wrong side of the lining strips. Roll to smooth into place, using a roller or rolling pin. Coat the entire wrong side of the straps, interfacing and all, with adhesive, and fold the long sides over, pounding as you work. Edge-stitch with matching thread down the length of the strips.

Place the straps face up on the right side of the lining material about halfway between the fold line and the edge of the lining. Turn the ends of the straps to the wrong side of the lining fabric, adhere them, pound firmly, and clamp until dry.

Then coat the wrong side of both needlework and lining lightly with adhesive. When it is tacky, align the two pieces, roll them together to smooth them out, pound the edges, and weight until dry. When they're dry, edge-stitch all around the four sides of the work with invisible thread. Fold the cover on the fold line and pound to set the fold. You may also, if you wish, stitch down the fold line with invisible thread to secure it.

If you prefer, use another procedure for this project. You can use woven fabric for the lining and ribbon for the straps, and bind the cover with bias binding or ribbon. Or you can use binding stitch all around, and place the lining just as in these instructions. In either case—whether you chose binding stitch or binding—you would omit the continental stitching.

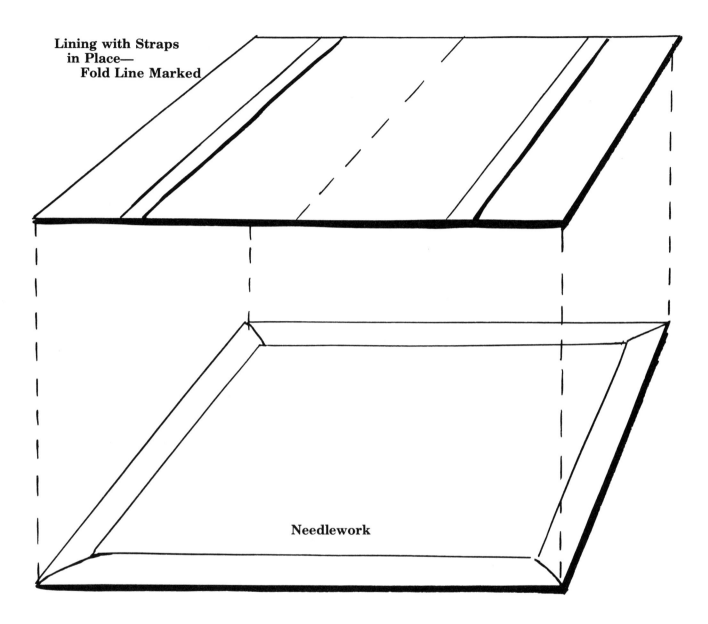

**Lining with Straps
in Place—
Fold Line Marked**

Needlework

Variations

Paperback Book Jackets: For this, make your needlework 7¾ inches high by 10½ inches wide; this should accommodate most newsstand-size paperbacks. Make just as you do the *TV Guide* cover, but use elastic in place of the straps, and make 2 folds to accommodate the spine of the book.

Cover for Top-Bound Checkbook: Most top-bound checkbooks will require needlework 6½ inches wide by 6¾ inches high. Make one lining piece the same size and two lining pieces each 6½ inches wide by 3 inches high. Assemble in this fashion:

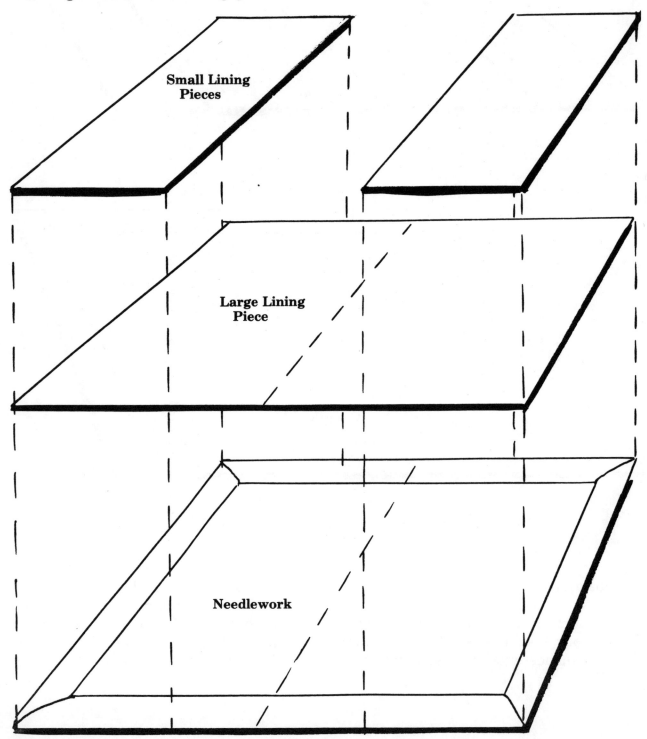

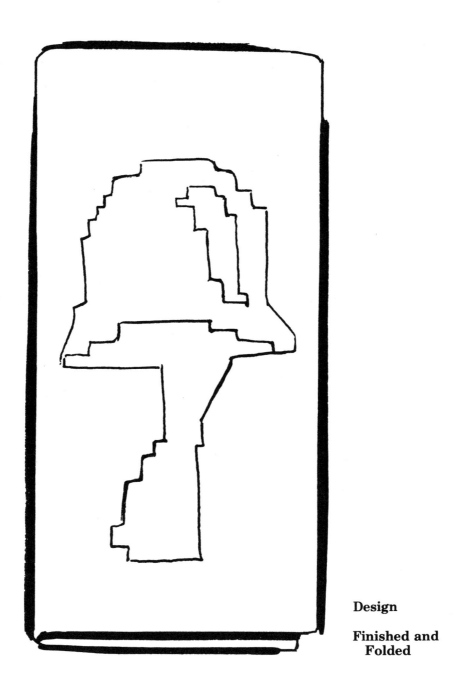

Design

**Finished and
Folded**

Make sure your design runs the right way—right side up across the bottom half of your needlework.

The bottom pocket will accommodate your checks, the top one your bank identification and credit cards.

Projects

Cover for Side-Bound Checkbook: This requires a piece of needlework about 3⅛ inches by 11½ inches, and one lining piece of the same dimensions, and one lining piece 3⅛ inches by 4 inches. You will also need a snap to fasten your checkbook cover.

Check the illustration, block out your needlework outline, fold canvas on fold lines, and mark snap placement. Do not work stitches in the area where snaps will be placed.

Treat this as you have the other projects in this section, but place the smaller lining piece a half inch from the left edge of the cover, as positioned in the sketch. Set ball part of snap in flap, and opposite side of snap in the back of the case, so that they come together perfectly; check positions before setting snaps.

**Pattern for Needlework Indicating
Fold Lines and Snap Placement**

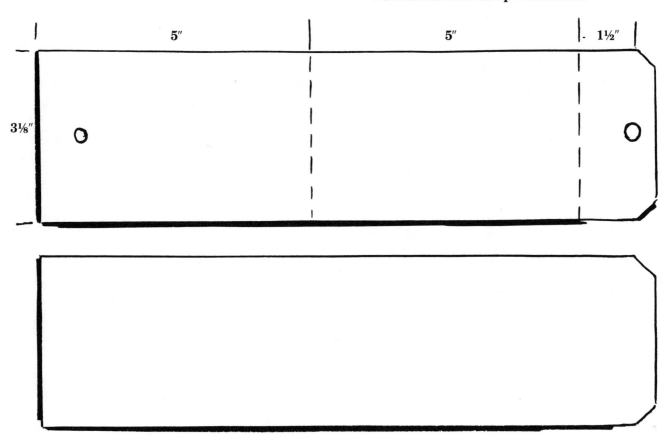

Lining 1, Same Dimensions as Needlework

Lining 2, through which you slip the cardboard checkbook backing, will hold your checks in place.

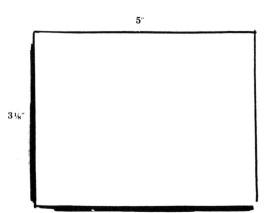

5"

3 ⅛"

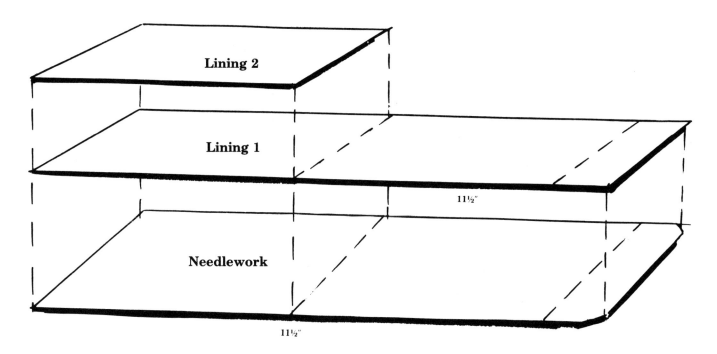

Lining 2

Lining 1

11½"

Needlework

11½"

**Folded and Finished,
Snaps in Place**

Projects

SCISSORS CASE: This is a fairly quick and handy case to make for most small embroidery scissors. Measure the length of your scissors and add one inch to the measurement; the sum will be your radius as you mark out a quarter circle on canvas, as below, using a ruler and an ordinary child's compass.

Complete your stitchery. Block, size, trim and reinforce. Miter the corner, and turn under the long edges, leaving a single thread visible on each side so you can join the two with binding stitch. Cut a piece of felt slightly smaller than the needlepoint and adhere it. Stitch felt to curved edge, just into needlework, and trim canvas even with stitching. Make and apply bias binding to the curved edge of the needlepoint, turning the ends under to be slip-stitched later on. Apply the snaps where marked.

Fold the needlepoint over, fasten the snap, and steam and pound to crease. Work binding stitch from the point to the edge of the bias binding, working the first stitches over one end of the yarn and finishing off by running the other end of the yarn under the stitching. Slip-stitch the ends of the bias binding with a curved needle and invisible thread.

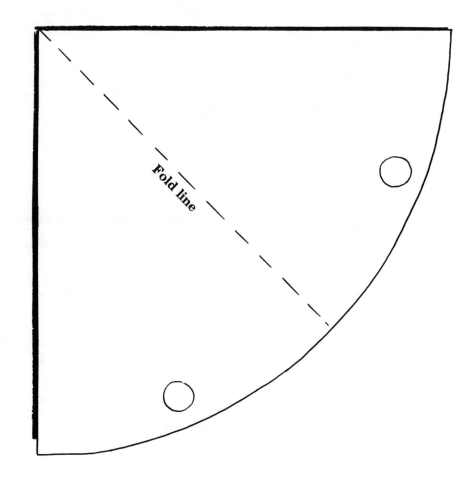

SCISSORS CASE 2: Here is another scissors case, different from the first and a bit more difficult to pull off. I would suggest 18 mesh canvas for this one, and advise that you make certain as you draw your pattern that each piece is perfectly symmetrical and that the two pieces match, mesh for mesh. You'll need a ⅜-inch snap (either the sew-on kind or the set-in kind), bias binding made from a 1-inch strip about 18 inches in length, and thread to match your bias binding, plus a small amount of fabric for lining.

Lay out your pattern, adapting it to the size of your own scissors. Complete your stitchery. Do not add continental stitch. Block, size, and trim. Cut two lining pieces, one the same size as each piece of needlework. Put each piece of lining with the appropriate piece of needlework, wrong sides facing, and stitch them together—working just into the needlework—on your sewing machine. Trim any excess lining and canvas right next to the edge of the needlework itself. Finish the top of piece A with bias binding If you are using set snaps, set them now.

Put the two pieces together, lining sides facing, and stitch around again. Then, starting from the bottom edge, apply bias binding all around, butting the ends as in the instructions for bias cording and binding (see page 36).

If you are using sew-on snaps, sew them into place.

Fasten your snaps, and steam and pound the fold line.

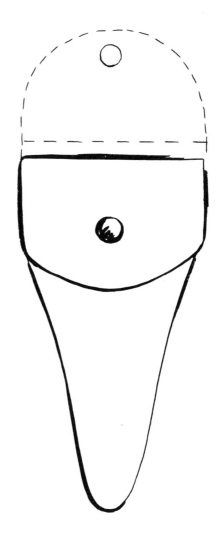

Projects

KEYCASE: For this you will need a piece of needlework 5¾ inches by 3½ inches, a ⅜-inch snap and setting tools, 3¼-inch rivets or eyelets, and one 6-hook key plate, Tandy item #1170.

Lay out your pattern, which will be similar to the above, eliminating stitches where each eyelet will go to fasten the plate to the inside of the case (it is shown here without the hooks for the sake of clarity), and omitting a small block of stitches to help you with snap placement later on.

Complete your stitchery. Add two rows of continental stitch all round.

Block, size, trim, and reinforce. Notch at fold lines. Miter corners, and turn excess canvas and continental stitch to the wrong side, steaming and pinning as you work. Pound. Cut lining material of light leather or Ultrasuede and adhere. Stitch needlework and lining together with invisible thread.

Place the key plate, and mark lining for hole placement. Cut holes, and use rivets or eyelets to fasten the plate. Fold on fold lines. Lap the sides to check snap placement. Place snaps.

Fasten snaps, and steam and pound to set fold line creases.

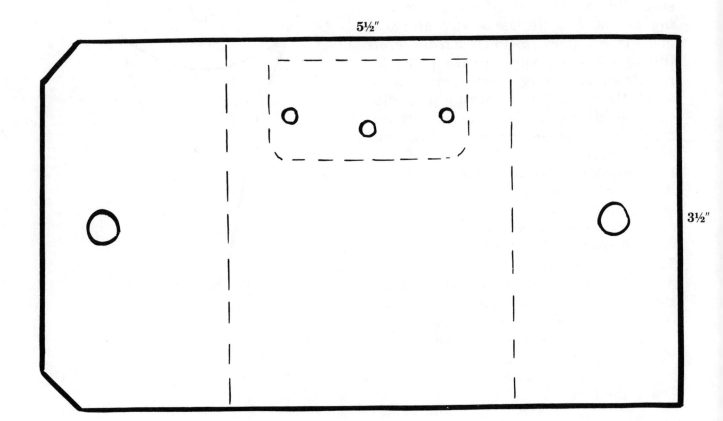

5½"

3½"

GLASSES CASES

Needlepoint glasses cases are attractive, of course, but they're practical too, for the firm padding of the needlework really protects both lenses and frames. We are including directions for three different styles, all of which are assembled in about the same way.

Before you lay out your pattern, make sure that your case will fit the pair of glasses for which it is destined; wrap the glasses loosely in paper to get a rough idea of the measurements. A man's horn-rims would demand a larger case than one for most women's glasses. Use small canvas, 16 or 18 mesh, for any case.

To make the cases, you'll need your needlework, lining and interfacing cut to the size of the needlework plus seam allowances, extra wool for the binding stitch, and invisible thread.

For each of the cases, make sure that you will have a mesh-for-mesh match when you start to put them together. If you select a pattern with folds, design your needlework to take best advantage of them. Complete your stitchery. Do not add continental stitch. Block, size, and trim. Working one thread out from the needlework, miter corners and turn back excess canvas to prepare it for binding stitch. Notch at the fold lines.

For the two-piece case, put the pieces wrong sides together, align them, and begin the binding stitch—catching one thread on each side, and thus stitching the two pieces together—at the point marked. As you work around to the other side, complete the joining work over the top of the uppermost piece, and finish off where you began. Turn the piece over and work binding stitch over the top of the other half.

Cut two pieces of interfacing slightly smaller than the finished needlework, place them on the wrong side of your lining fabric, and turn and baste the fabric seam allowances back over them. Place the two lining pieces right sides together and stitch them up the sides, to correspond with the needlework. Slip the lining into the need-

Glasses Cases

Two-Piece

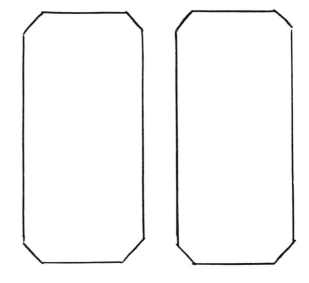

Projects

lework and slip-stitch the lining and the needlework together at the top with invisible thread.

For the one-piece foldover, fold to align perfectly, begin where marked, join the two sides as far as the angle, then bind the edge of the top half and continue around the fold to cover the edge until you meet the joined portion. Make and insert the lining for this case just as you would for the two-piece case.

For the long one-piece foldover, fold the piece and begin the stitching where marked. Use the binding stitch to join front and back, then across the top of the lower flap, and then the joining on the right side. Return to the left side, where you turned that first corner, and bind the entire flap. Make and apply the lining as in the previous directions, and fasten with a frog-and-button closing or a snap.

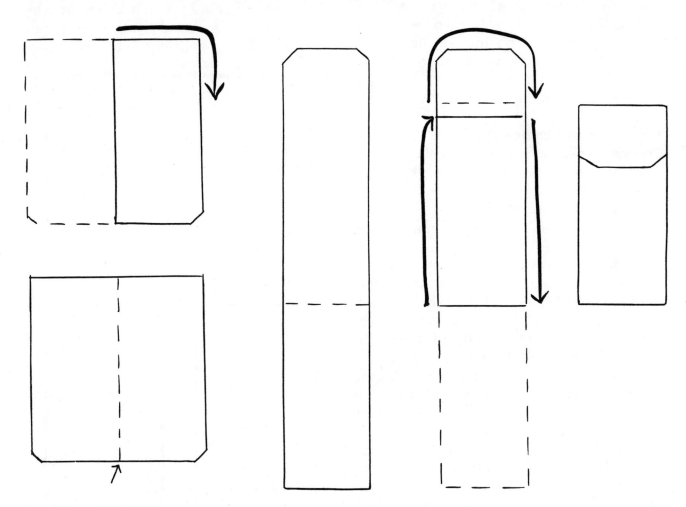

One-Piece Side Fold

One-Piece Double Fold

BILLFOLD

For this you will need a piece of needlework about 9¼ inches by 3⅜ inches; heavy-duty invisible thread; sewing-machine needles designed for sewing leather; leather adhesive or craft glue; a pounding block or cobbler's hammer; and enough Ultrasuede to make one piece 9¼ by 3⅜ inches (the backlining) and one 9¾ by 2⅝ inches (the inside).

Using canvas 14 mesh or smaller, outline your project and draw your pattern, making sure that it will be as effective when your billfold is folded as it is when the piece is opened out flat.

Complete your needlework and make two rows of continental stitching all around; block, size, trim, and reinforce. Miter corners, and using your iron and plenty of steam, turn back the excess canvas and the continental stitching; pound to flatten the crease.

With leather adhesive or craft glue, coat the inside of both the billfold back lining and the wrong side of the needlework. When the adhesive is tacky, align the pieces, put them together, smooth them out with a roller or rolling pin, pound them lightly around the edges, and weight them. Allow them to dry.

When they have dried, take the billfold inside and hold the piece against the lined needlework. The bottom and side edges of the billfold inside should line up with the bottom and side edges of the lining; the top edge of the inside will be free, making a pocket for your bills.

The edges that line up must be adhered, then sewn. Adhere them as before, using just a thin line of leather adhesive or craft glue on the edges of the pieces. Align them, put them to-

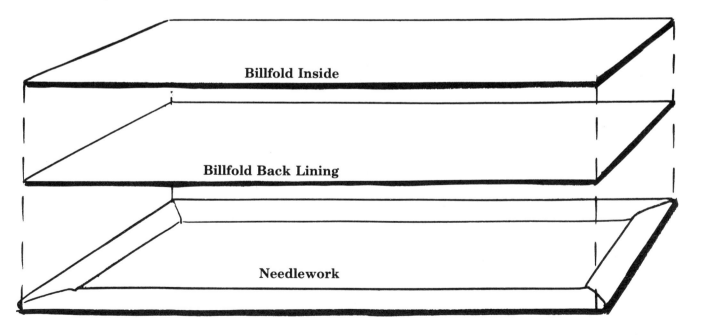

Billfold Inside

Billfold Back Lining

Needlework

gether, pound them, and clamp them into place until dry.

Then, using a leather needle and invisible thread in your sewing machine, use the zipper foot to stitch all four sides of the work. This will secure the lining to the needlework along the top, and the lining, needlework, and inside on the other three sides.

If you want a strap-and-snap closing, make and apply it as in the directions for the passport case.

JEWELRY ROLL

A roll that will accommodate your jewelry and stockings, plus other tiny odds and ends, can tuck handily in a corner of your suitcase and keep everything from scattering. It also makes a very special gift. Our preference for making it would be bargello on 16 mesh canvas and a lining of garment-weight leather or suede.

You'll need the following: About 3 square feet of leather or a half yard of Ultrasuede; a small piece of medium woven interfacing; one grommet and one snap, plus a hole puncher and setting tools; a roller or rolling pin and a pounder or cobbler's hammer; invisible thread and leather needles for your sewing machine; three 7-inch zippers and thread to match your lining material; masking tape; and a piece of needlepoint made to the large measurements (outside line) of the pattern.

First, the needlework. Outline your pattern on canvas, marking center lines and grommet placement. Do your stitch-

ery, omitting grommet area, and add 2 rows of continental stitch all around. Block, size, trim, and reinforce. Miter corners, press the excess canvas and continental stitching to the wrong side, and pound, using plenty of steam.

Cut a piece of your lining material to the same dimensions as your needlework. Coat the wrong sides of both needlework and lining material with adhesive; when it is tacky, align the pieces, put them together, roll them with a roller or rolling pin to smooth them out, pound them, and weight them with a heavy book until dry. Cut the hole, place the grommet, and set the piece aside.

Now cut two pieces of your lining material to the measurements of the needlework. In one of the pieces, cut the openings marked as zipper openings.

Take this piece, some masking tape, and your zippers (press the zippers flat first). Lay the zippers on the wrong side of the lining piece so that the right sides of the zippers show through the openings. The zipper *tapes* will lie on the wrong side, on either side of the cutout and slightly overlapping the ends of the cutout. Tape the zippers from the back with masking tape; from the front, sew them in place, using a leather needle, the zipper foot, and matching thread. Strip the masking tape away from the back of the work.

Now cut two straps from the strap pattern (outer lines) and two pieces of interfacing from the interfacing pattern (inner lines). Place and adhere the interfacing against the wrong side of the lining material as indicated in the pattern,

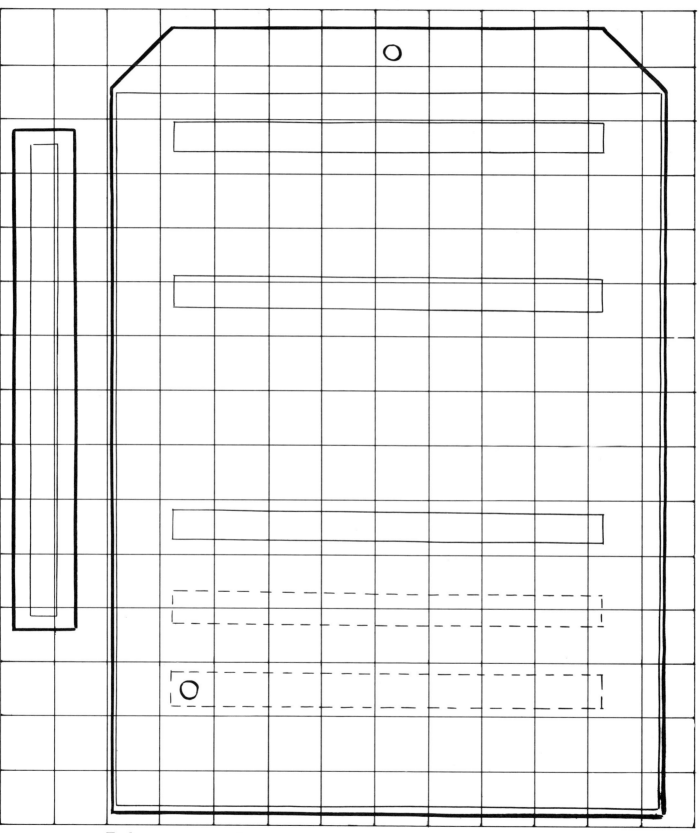

**Each square represents
1 inch.**

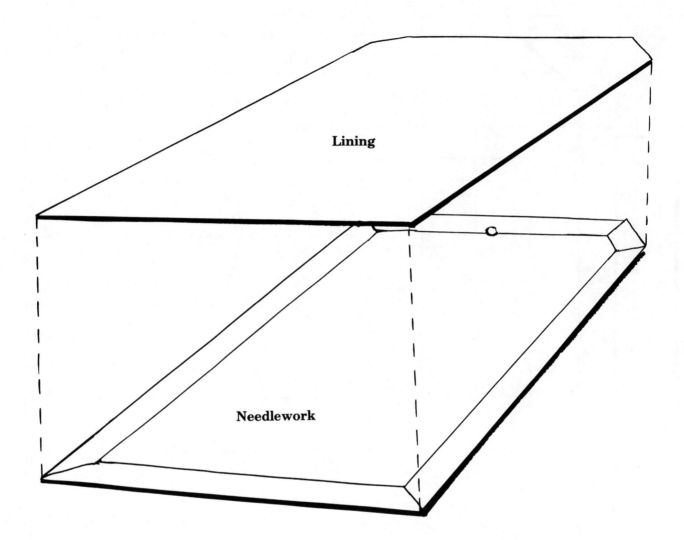

Lining

Needlework

**Put needlework and
lining together.
Place grommet.**

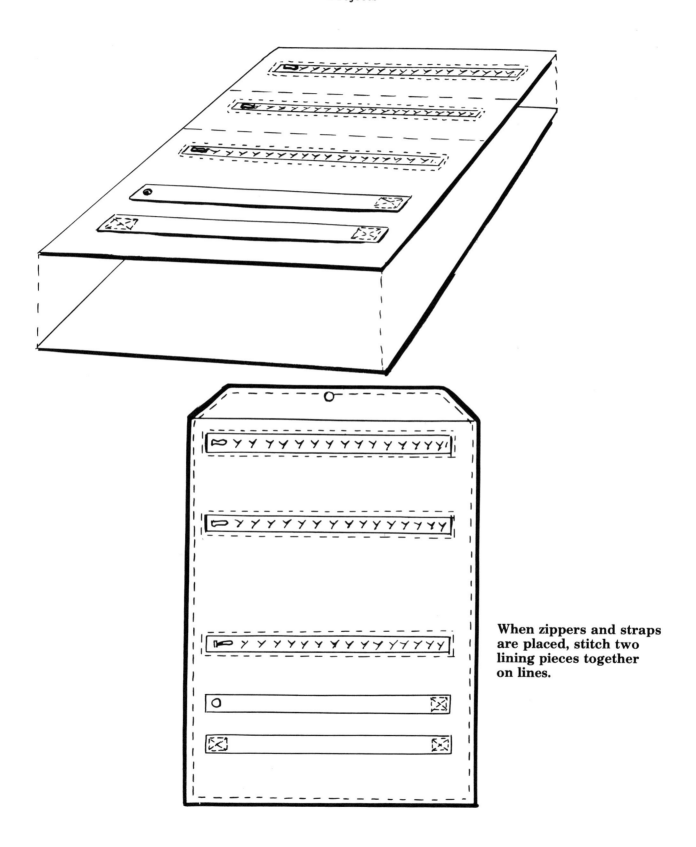

When zippers and straps are placed, stitch two lining pieces together on lines.

and fold the long sides over and adhere them, too. Roll, pound, and weight. Edge-stitch all around the straps, using the zipper foot and matching thread.

One strap, for earrings, will be sewn into place on both ends. Place it as indicated in the pattern. Tape it in place with a bit of masking tape; on the wrong side, reinforce the ends with small pieces of interfacing, also taped in place. Then sew firmly, using matching thread, like this:

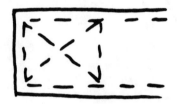

The other strap, for rings, has a snap at one end. Place the ball portion of the snap in one end:

Now align the strap as indicated in the pattern, and sew the other end in place just as you did for the first strap—masking tape, reinforcement, and all. Press the snap down to leave a slight impression that will help you position the other half of the snap exactly. Set that part of the snap in, reinforcing on the wrong side with a bit of interfacing.

Courage! You're almost done.

Now line up and place the two pieces together. Hold them in place with masking tape while you stitch. Stitch straight across, side to side, at the top edge and along two lines even with the *top* line of stitching on each zipper. Careful! Use the illustration as a guide. This makes your pockets. Remove the masking tape.

Place the pocket section against the lined needlework. Adhere with a thin line of adhesive on the edges, pound, and weight until dry. Then edge-stitch all around, as indicated in the illustration, as close to the edge as you can. When you've done this, it remains only to place the grommet, and to make a slipknot through it of macrame cord, twisted cord made of spare wool, or ribbon. A few feet will be about the right length to wrap and tie around your case, and gives it a perfect finishing touch.

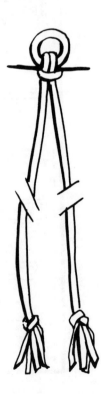

TEA COZY

This is the only kitchen item we know of that you might actually want to make in needlepoint.

You will need enough ready-made quilted fabric for a lining.

To begin, measure horizontally across the fattest part of your teapot, from the tip of the spout to the end of the handle. Add two inches on each side and you have the width of your pattern, which includes seam allowances. Mea-sure the height and double it, which gives you the height of your pattern, including seam allowances. This formula works well for standard shapes of teapots. If yours happens to be extremely tall and thin, don't double the height measurement; simply add an inch or two to the height to give a pleasing shape to the tea cozy. Lay out your dimensions on graph paper and connect the lines so that you have an attractive shape. We provide a pattern for a standard Brown Betty English Teapot to give you an idea.

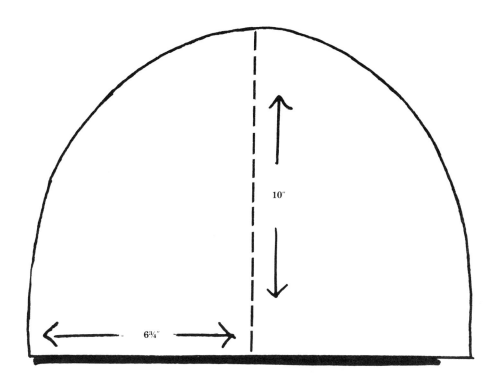

6¾"

10″

Make sure that the widest part of the finished cozy will fall at the widest part of your teapot. Trace your pattern twice on the same piece of canvas, with the tracings four inches apart. Draw your design on the pieces. Let your imagination run riot on this. You can do one that is terribly proper, with posies on it, or do an animal design, with one side of the cozy representing the front of the animal and the other side its back. Or you can do what our tea-drinking friend Teri Hassid did and make a teapot cozy with three-dimensional spout and handle.

Complete your needlework and block it. Stitch just inside needlework on your sewing machine. Cut out two pattern pieces from quilted fabric, using your needlepoint pattern pieces.

With right sides facing, sew needle-point pieces together. Clip and grade seams.

If you are planning to add three-dimensional pieces to your design, such as ears, tails, or spouts and handles, you should do this before you sew the needlepoint pieces together. Work your extra pieces on separate pieces of canvas. Stitch just into needlework with your machine, then cut away excess canvas. With wrong sides facing, whipstitch together with yarn. Then stuff with polyester batting. Baste in place on one main needlepoint piece, making sure it is on the inside while you are sewing seams together, so that when you turn the cozy right side out, everything will be in its proper place.

Now, with right sides facing, sew lining pieces together three-quarters of the way up on each side like this:

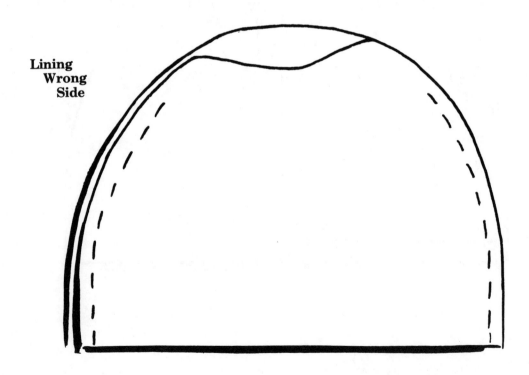

Lining
Wrong
Side

With right sides facing, place lining
over needlepoint.

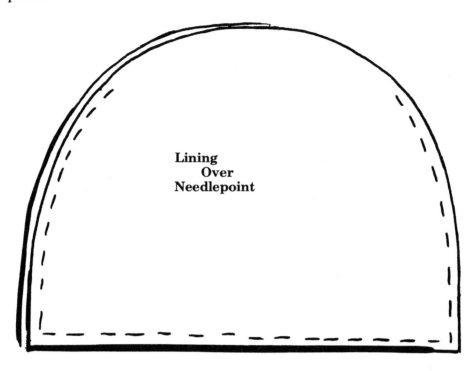

**Lining
Over
Needlepoint**

Sew bottom seam closed. Pull needlepoint through hole left in lining seam.

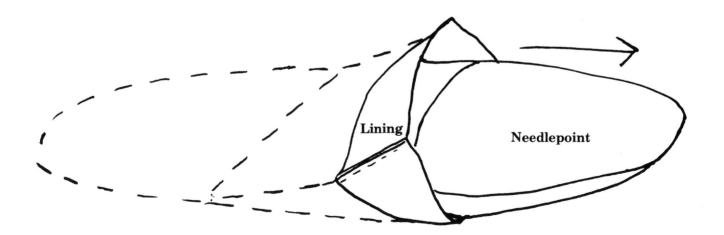

Lining

Needlepoint

Close seam in lining by hand. Turn lining to inside of needlepoint.

**Stitch by hand.
Right Sides Out**

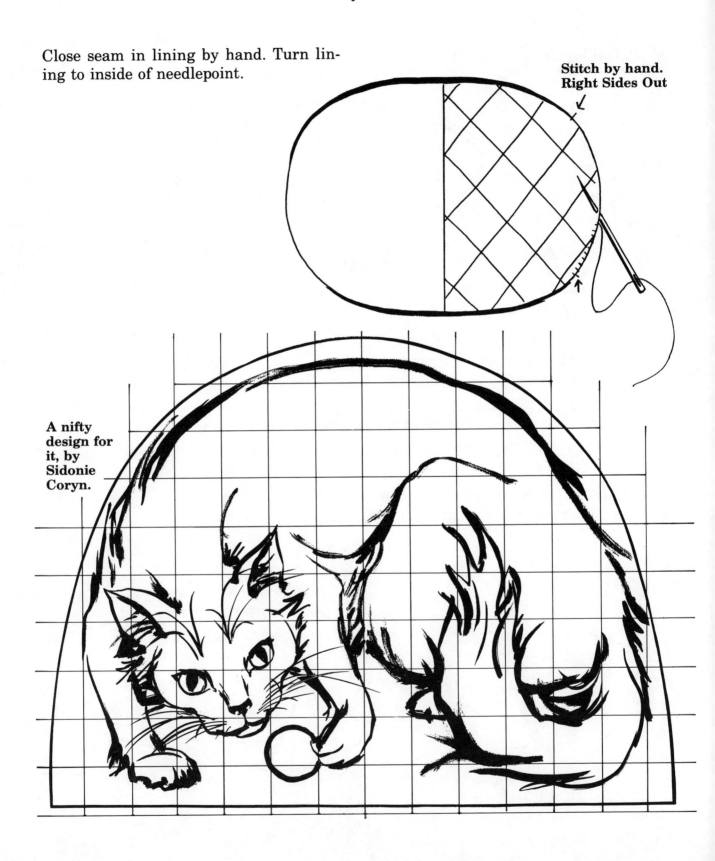

**A nifty
design for
it, by
Sidonie
Coryn.**

TOBACCO POUCH

Pipe smokers love this. There is really more pouch than needlepoint, but it's personalized and it really keeps tobacco fresh. We like this done in brown Ultrasuede, suede, or vinyl, with a needlepoint insert done on 14 or 18 mesh canvas. A masculine monogram worked in black lettering on a beige background is very handsome.

Here are some pointers on sewing vinyl and leather:

1. Use mercerized cotton thread.

2. You will not be able to use pins because the holes they leave behind are permanent. Use transparent tape or masking tape.

3. You will not be able to press seams open. Press seams open with your fingers, and then, if you like, glue the seam allowances flat, using rubber cement. Apply the cement to the two surfaces to be glued together, and when the cement is tacky, stick them together and then pound with a wooden clapper or mallet.

You will need two pieces of outer material measuring 8 inches by 6 inches, which allows for a half-inch seam allowance all around and gives you a finished pouch measuring 7 inches by 5 inches. Buy a 7-inch zipper and enough polyurethane plastic sheeting to make two pieces 8 inches by 6 inches for the lining. You can buy this at hardware stores, and after you cut out these two pieces, you will have enough left over to cover your car! Buy the kind that is several mils thick.

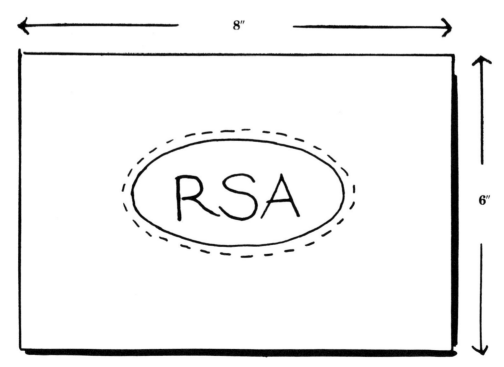

Tobacco Pouch

Using one of the outside pieces, make the cutout for the monogram insert. We don't think it should be too large or it will begin to look like a lady's purse. A small oval centered in the piece looks well.

The easiest way to make the oval or circle (or square, for that matter) perfect is to make a cardboard cutout of the shape you want and cut around it carefully with a sharp mat knife.

Line up your canvas neatly behind the cutout, making sure that the squares are straight up and down. Hold the canvas in place with masking tape on the back. Working carefully from the front, stitch close to the raw edges of the cutout, using long stitches. Trace the monogram or the design onto the canvas, then do your needlework in the basket-weave stitch so it will not get out of shape. Work as far up to the edge of the cutout as you can.

Fold back seam allowances on top edge of outside leather pieces. Press seam flat with your fingers and glue seam allowances flat with rubber cement. Place folded edges together like this:

**Place folded
edges together.**

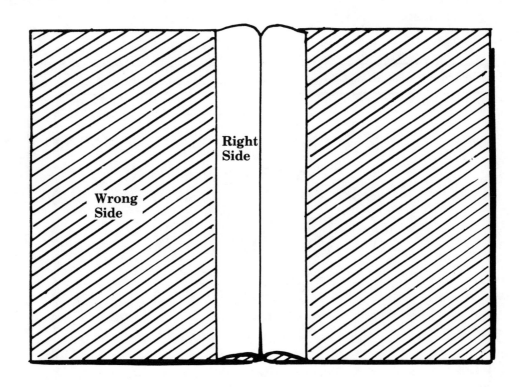

Right Side

Wrong Side

Edges should be just touching each other. Working from the right side, tape the two pieces together. This will be your zipper seam.

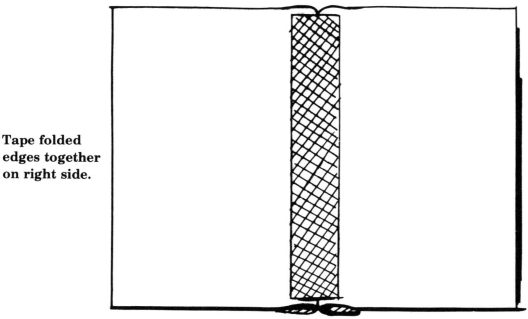

Tape folded edges together on right side.

Working from the wrong side, place zipper face down along the seam line and tape it in place, making sure that tape will not be caught in the seam by placing it toward outside edge of zipper tape.

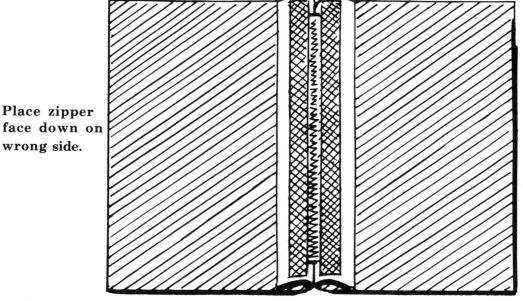

Place zipper face down on wrong side.

Apply tape on outer edges of zipper tape in order to hold it in place.

Projects

Fold back seam allowances of top edges of inside plastic lining pieces. Press seam flat with your fingers and glue in place. Place folded edges of lining pieces along zipper tape on inside of pouch. Don't position it too near the zipper teeth or it will get caught when the pouch is opened and closed. Tape lining pieces in place by putting tape at a right angle to the zipper.

Sew zipper to these points.

Place lining on zipper and place at right angles to hold lining in place.

Sew zipper to these points.

Sew zipper in place, taking care to sew only to the exact start and finish of the zipper teeth, keeping side seam allowances free on outside leather pieces and on lining. With right sides together, sew sides of outer material, folding zipper tape in half so that you can catch the ends of the zipper tape in the seam. With right sides of lining material together sew side seams. Open zipper. With right sides together, sew bottom seam of outer material closed. Turn pouch right side out. Pull lining to outside and sew bottom seam by hand, or, with seam allowances turned under and facing each other, sew seam on your machine. Turn lining to inside.

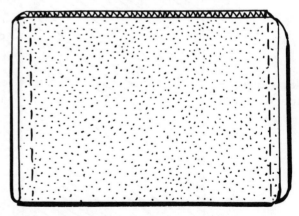

With right sides together, sew side seams of outside material, catching zipper tape in seam, keeping lining out of your way. Then, sew lining side seams in the same manner.
Open zipper and sew bottom seam of outside material.

Finished Pouch

This method of inserting needlepoint into other materials can be adapted to many uses. If you decide to use it on fabrics other than leather, Ultrasuede, or vinyl, it should be very firm so that it will have as much body as the needlepoint insert. Also, the edges of the cutout will have to be finished so that they will not ravel. You will have to make a facing for the cutout, which you do by duplicating the cutout on a piece of fabric, placing cutouts one on top of another, right sides together, and sewing all around. Clip corners or curves and grade seam allowances all around. Turn facing to the inside and press flat. It will be kept in place by the stitching used to insert the needlepoint canvas.

The methods used for the tobacco pouch can also be used to make a very attractive makeup case. You might try making the insert quite large for this. The insert is attractive as a monogram with flowers around it.

PASSPORT CASE

Like so many things, this looks harder to do than it actually is. Really, if some of the things we've made so far are put together rather like sandwiches, this is somewhat like a club sandwich—the same, but with more layers. And since, for anyone who travels, it is both useful and elegant, it is very much worth doing.

For this you'll need a piece of needlework 7⅝ inches by 9⅜ inches. Lay it out, and mark where you'll be setting the snaps so you will know where to omit stitching. You'll also need invisible thread and thread to match your lining, leather needles for your sewing machine, ⅜-inch snaps and setting tools to place them with, small pieces of interfacing, adhesive and a roller or rolling pin, a cobbler's hammer or pounding block, and enough lightweight leather of Ultrasuede to make the following:

1 lining piece 7⅝ by 9⅜ inches
1 lining piece 7⅜ by 9⅜ inches
2 lining pieces 4⅜ by 7⅜ inches
2 lining pieces 3⅞ by 7⅜ inches
2 lining pieces 3⅜ by 7⅜ inches
2 strap pieces 1⅛ by 3 inches

It will be easier to lay these out if you mark them first on 8-to-the-inch graph paper and then stack them in the order indicated on the pattern. Once you've done this, you'll see just how everything goes together.

First of all, complete your stitchery, add two rows of continental stitch all around, block, size, trim, and reinforce. Miter corners, and turn back excess canvas and continental stitch. Pound the turns and catch-stitch or adhere the seam allowances in place. Take your largest lining piece and coat the wrong sides of both lining and needlework with adhesive; when the adhesive is tacky, align the pieces, put them together, roll to smooth them out, pound, and weight.

Take the strap pieces and cut a piece of interfacing slightly smaller to sandwich between them. Adhere the

pieces, wrong sides together, pound, edge-stitch, and sew in place on the needlework as indicated. Place the ball portion of a snap on the strap as shown; place the two socket ends of the snaps, reinforced with a bit of interfacing, as shown to correspond—two closings to permit the user to close the case even when it's stuffed with the odds and ends of travel. Set aside the needlework, now lined and with its fasteners in place, while you work on the pocket section, into which all that travel paraphernalia will eventually go.

Have your lining pieces stacked as in the pattern drawing. Take up the two top pieces on the left, put them together with masking tape, and stitch with matching thread, as indicated, to make two pockets. Peel the tape away, and replace the two pieces on the left-hand stack.

Take up the top piece on the right, and, reinforcing with a scrap of interfacing, place a ball portion of a snap where indicated; this will hold a case of traveler's checks slipped down into the large pocket. When you've set the snap, line up this piece with the next one, tape them together as you did the pieces from the left side, and stitch them into thirds as indicated. Replace these pieces on the right-hand stack.

Now, taking each piece in turn, rim just inside the edges with a thin line of adhesive where the stitching lines will fall; line up the pieces, and put them together for the entire pocket section of the case, just as in the layout. Roll, pound, and weight. Edge-stitch with

Passport-case pattern, layout, and stitching guide. See also reverse.

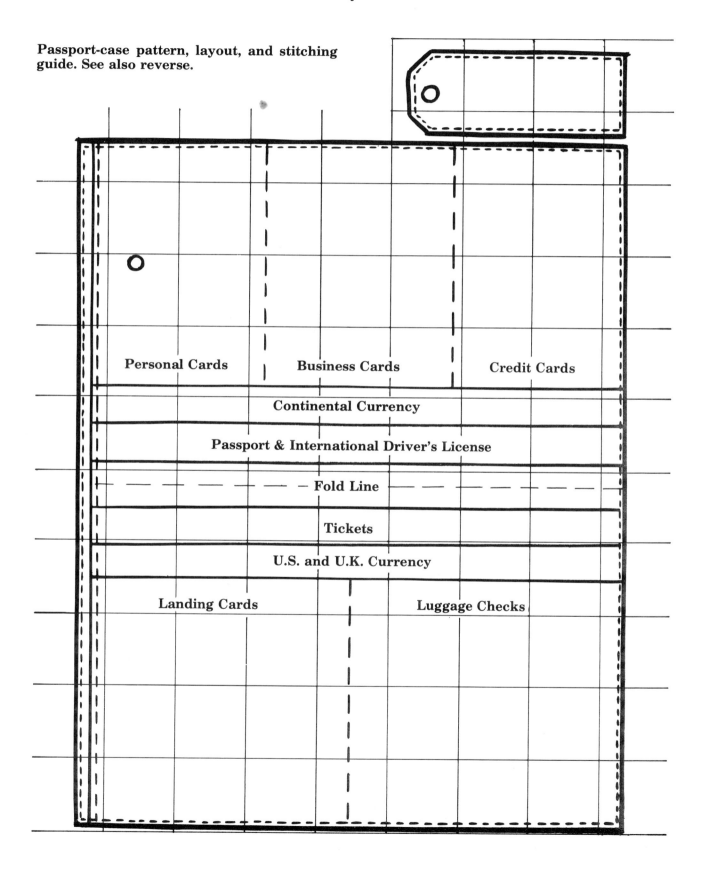

Personal Cards — Business Cards — Credit Cards

Continental Currency

Passport & International Driver's License

Fold Line

Tickets

U.S. and U.K. Currency

Landing Cards — Luggage Checks

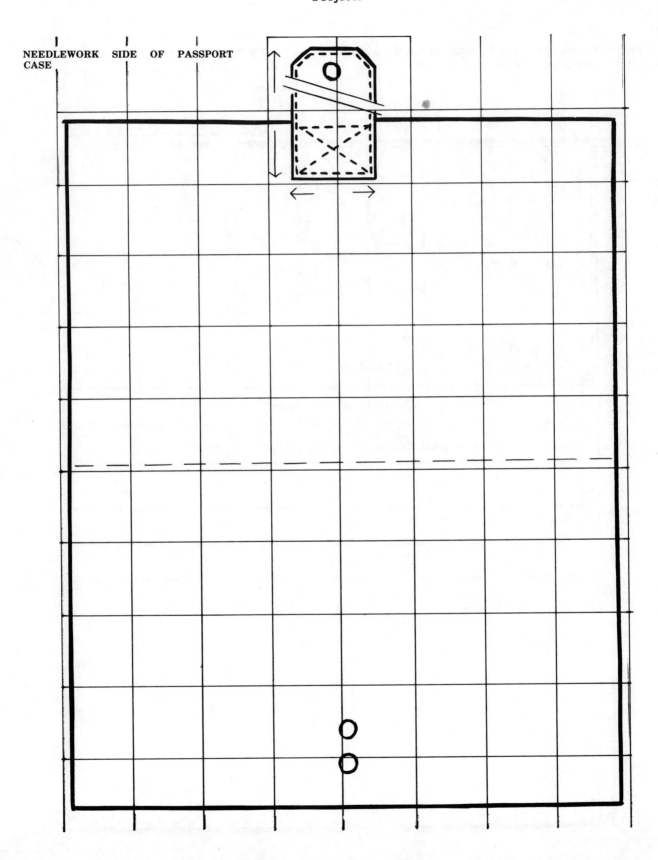

NEEDLEWORK SIDE OF PASSPORT
CASE

matching thread across the top of the pocket section only.

Then adhere the edges of the pocket section to the edges of the needlepoint lining, using the same procedure. With invisible thread, edge-stitch around all four sides. Fold the case on the fold-line, steam and pound to set the crease, fasten the strap, and you're done.

It took a while, but it's great-looking, isn't it?

Needlepoint for Wearing Apparel and Accessories

Following are instructions for a man's cummerbund and a man's or woman's vest. The vest is a tricky project and you should be sure to spend all the time necessary measuring, planning and making a muslin so that the final result will be not only beautiful but *wearable*. We have seen skirts made of needlepoint and this is possible because you wash the finished needlepoint and soften it so that the result is a fabric about the weight of winter woolens. The idea does not appeal to us somehow but if you would like to try a skirt or some other article of clothing in needlepoint proceed as you would for the vest; using a commercial pattern, making a muslin and fitting it perfectly and so on. It would be horrible to do a large piece only to find that you have done it in the wrong size.

Rules for using needlepoint for wearing apparel:

1. Avoid the use of red, snow white, and black yarn in your work, as the colors will run and *everything* will bleed into white.

2. Do your stitchery so that the piece needs no blocking.

3. When you are finished with your stitchery, edge-stitch just into the needlework with your sewing machine.

4. Immerse the piece for 30 seconds in cold water and Woolite.

5. Rinse thoroughly in cold water. Blot.

6. Pin out over several thicknesses of toweling.

7. Let dry, and assemble your garment.

CUMMERBUND

Use a commercial pattern and buckle. Cut the sides of the cummerbund from satin, and also cut a lining for the needlework from satin.

For the center front piece of the cummerbund, place the pattern piece (make all folds with the paper pattern) on your canvas according to the sewing instructions; you may use it either straight, or, preferably, on the bias. Use the paper pattern to trace the outline for your needlepoint. Be sure to leave 3 or 4 inches of blank canvas all around.

Lay out your design, and complete your stitchery. This project is very effective when worked in bargello. Block and stitch around on your sewing machine, using a narrow zigzag that takes you just inside the stitching. Continue assembly in accord with the pattern instructions.

MAN'S OR WOMAN'S VEST

For this you will need a commercial vest pattern, a number of decorative set snaps instead of buttons, satin for the back, and lining and leather binding.

Begin by making and fitting a muslin replica of the vest you want, *minus* pockets, which are nearly impossible to fit into a needlework vest. Transfer any alterations to your paper pattern, and use the paper pattern to mark out your outlines for your needlepoint on canvas 14 mesh or smaller, including darts, and snap placement. The smaller the canvas, the more detail you will be able to incorporate into your design and the more flexible the vest fabric will be. To do the marking, use blue dressmaker's carbon paper and a plain (unserrated) tracing wheel. Go over the marks with a waterproof felt-tip marker, making just a dot to indicate snap placements. As you work your stitchery you'll leave the dots free of stitching to help you later with placement.

Work out your design, being sure to match pattern perfectly on all pieces, and cut out the canvas pieces—remembering to leave 3 or 4 inches of canvas around all the pieces—and do your stitchery. When you've finished, block and stitch around your pieces with the

sewing machine, just into the stitchery. Trim the seam allowances away on the free edges, like this:

First stitch darts, if your pattern has them, and then the seams. Bind the free edges with leather or (easier) premade bias binding. Set snaps in place.

Assemble the back of the vest according to the pattern instructions, and line either the entire vest or the front with satin.

DOG COATS

We mention this item in passing since there are many dogs and dog owners who cannot live without them. Our best advice would be to use a commercial pattern, but we have looked high and low and can't find one, so until such time as the pattern companies decide to print one, your best bet is to use an existing coat as a pattern, tracing the outline onto tracing paper and transferring all markings for snaps, etc. If you don't already own a dog coat, you must

Projects

measure the dog, from his collar to the base of his tail, and then stroll into your local pet store and ask them—if you have enough nerve—if they will let you trace a dog coat in the size you need.

Be sure to keep the style simple, to make certain the needlepoint pattern is symmetrical from the center back down both sides, that you use heavy-duty snaps (available from Tandy), that you soften the coat by washing, as with the vest, line it with cotton, and bind with ½-inch commercial bias binding.

CLOGS

You will need to purchase clog bottoms and shoe nails, both of which are available from Tandy (see mail-order section of this book), and enough commercial bias binding to finish all edges.

The diagram of the clog pattern is for the right foot. The longer side goes on the outside of your foot. Trace the pattern, then flip it over and trace it for the left foot. Lay out the patterns on the same piece of canvas, 4 inches apart.

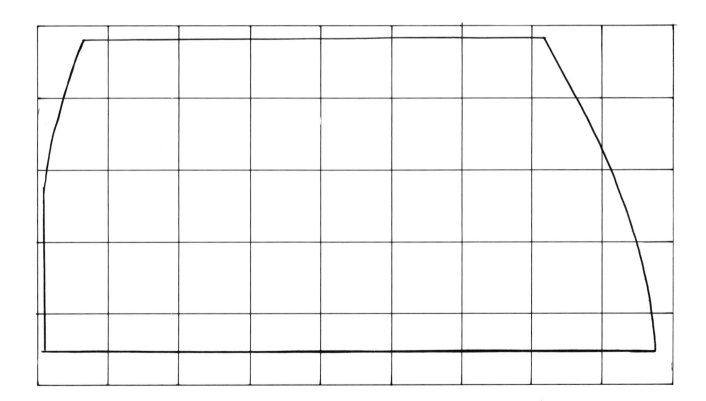

Clog pattern—right Foot

Each square represents 1 inch.

Projects

Work out your design. Trim away all excess canvas and apply bias binding to all unfinished edges. Do your stitchery. If you use a basket-weave stitch, the back of the work will be very comfortable to wear because it will be padded and smooth. No knots please! Block the finished pieces, but do not size them. Attach the finished canvas pieces to the clog bottoms, using shoe nails, unfinished clog bottoms should first be sanded, stained, and varnished, for a truly finished look.

N.B. Since this pattern fits Pat's 7½A, you might want to try yours in felt first, fitting it to clog bottoms with masking tape. Add or subtract for a perfect fit.

SKATING HAT

This skating hat, sized for women and girls, is copied from one that Pat's mother bought for her in Sweden many years ago. It's a good introduction to making clothing, in addition to being pretty and warm in any wind or weather.

Trace the center piece and the right-side piece onto 14 mesh canvas. Reverse the right-side piece to make the left side. You can use just the outlines and make your own pattern within them, or you can copy the whole thing.

Do your stitchery, but do not add any continental stitch. Block and trim, leaving half-inch seam allowances all around. Reinforce the seam lines in the canvas and the lines that will make the edges of the hat into the first two rows of needlepoint.

Notch and clip the seam line seam allowances as necessary, and press them to the back of the work along the seam lines. Pin the pieces to a tailor's ham or an inexpensive styrofoam wig stand, and slip-stitch them together with a curved needle and invisible thread. Be sure you match the symbols.

Make lining pieces from cotton or wool; when you purchase your fabric, make sure you get enough to make bias binding for the outside edges of the hat. Mark them and cut them to correspond with the pieces of the hat, leaving ample seam allowances. Using matching thread and a straight stitch on your sewing machine, sew the seam together, notching and clipping as necessary. Press the seams flat, and then press them open; this will be easier to do over a tailor's ham or a wig block padded with toweling to protect from the heat of the iron.

Pin the lining into the hat, wrong sides together, so that the lining fits smoothly in place. Sandwich two lengths of grosgrain or velvet ribbon between the lining and the needlework, as indicated on the pattern; these will be your ties. Now sew lining, needlework, and ties together, using the zigzag stitch on your sewing machine. Work close to the edge all around the edges, in the area that will later be covered by bias binding. Trim excess lining material and canvas even with the needlework, and don't let your attention wander when you do it. You don't want to cut the ties off!

Projects

Cut 1-inch bias strips, or use commercial bias binding, and make and apply bias binding, beginning and ending the application at the center back of the hat. The binding will roll right over the ribbon ties and reinforce them.

**Pattern for Skating Hat, Center.
Match symbols o and *. Add seam
allowance.
For lining, use same pattern pieces. Light
lines mark 1-inch squares. Dotted lines (next page)
indicate position for ties.
Choose bright primary
colors and a black
background.**

Skating Hat sides
Black Background

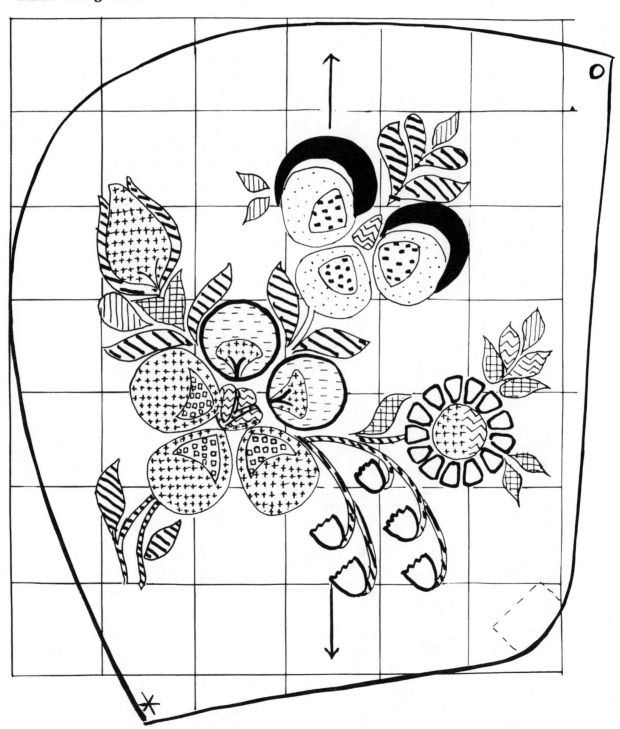

CLUTCH

Here is a small envelope-shaped clutch bag, which you can make in just about any size. This one, with the needlepoint 8 inches wide by 12¼ inches long down the center, is right for an evening bag; in a smaller size it would make a purse accessory. Whatever size you make it, these proportions would be just about correct.

To make it you'll need your needlework, a piece of interfacing the same size, a piece of fabric the same size plus seam allowances, a ⅜-inch snap of either the sew-on or the set-in sort, and invisible thread.

Lay out your stitchery for your chosen outline and mark off the fold lines. Plan your design to take best advantage of fold lines, and plan also for matching at the edge of the flap. Mark snap placements to omit a stitch; it will aid in placing them properly later on. Complete your stitchery and add two rows of continental stitch all around; block, size, trim, and reinforce. Notch at the fold lines, miter corners, and turn excess canvas and continental stitching to the wrong side. Catch-stitch or adhere in place after you have steamed and pounded the creases.

Trim the interfacing very narrowly—about 1/16 inch off each edge. Then lay it on the wrong side of your lining fabric, and turn back the lining seam allowances around it, mitering corners as necessary, Fold it on the fold lines, and stitch the side seams by hand.

Fit the lining to the needlework piece, slip-stitch the flap pieces together,

and fold the lower part of the needlework up to correspond with the lining. Steam and press the fold lines and set the snaps. Slip-stitch the lining and the needlework together where they meet under the flap. With the sewing machine and invisible thread, and the flap of the clutch open, edge-stitch the side seams.

You can vary this in numerous ways—in size, of course, or by substituting a frog closing for the snap closing, by making gussets for the sides if you're a fairly accomplished seamstress, by using binding stitch for the side seams, or whatever you'd like.

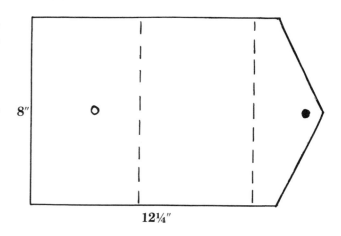

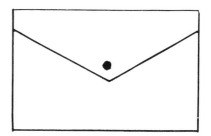

Projects

Making the frog of a frog and ball closing. The other side runs the opposite way.

Frog Closings: Since it is difficult to put buttonholes in needlework, frog closings are very handy to know about for garments, handbags, and so on. Make them, and the ball buttons that go with them, of purchased narrow braid or of self-filled or corded tubing. Both look best if you keep the seam line toward you as you form them, on what will be the wrong side of the work.

For the frogs, it is helpful to work on a piece of wide masking tape as you shape them. Stitch the ends together, and stitch as inconspicuously as possible where the tubing crosses itself; apply them with slip-stitch as invisibly as you can.

The ball buttons are a sort of macrame. Follow the diagram for tying them, pull the ends slowly and shape the little ball to form the button, then clip the ends short and sew them to the back of the button. If this seems unduly complicated, use regular purchased ball buttons.

The finished frog-and-button closing will look like this on a garment:

and like this on the flap of a handbag:

A few yard-goods stores stock frogs and buttons in various sizes and colors, but most of the time, to get a good color match, you'll find it better to make your own.

Make use of commercial pattern books to give you other ideas for clutch bags.

Miscellaneous Projects

RUGS

A needlepoint rug is the largest project you're likely to tackle, and since it's apt to become something of a family heirloom, we'd suggest that this is one time you shouldn't spare the expense. Buy the best quality of canvas and wool you can afford, and be painstaking with the design, laying it out completely on full-size sheets of paper. If your artistic talents fall short of something as elaborate as this, it is well worth investing in custom design. Considering the time you'll spend working on the rug, and the time you'll spend living with it, you'll certainly want it to be as nearly perfect as possible.

Rather than use big, ravelly 4 or 5 mesh rug canvas, we suggest 7, 8, or 10 mesh canvas, either monocanvas or penelope. If you are making a pieced rug, all the canvas must be from the same bolt, and each piece must be matched mesh for mesh. The job of putting the pieces together, we think, is best accomplished by a professional. Doing it yourself is tedious and frustrating, and it's agony if you mess up the job, whether you're working with plain squares like this:

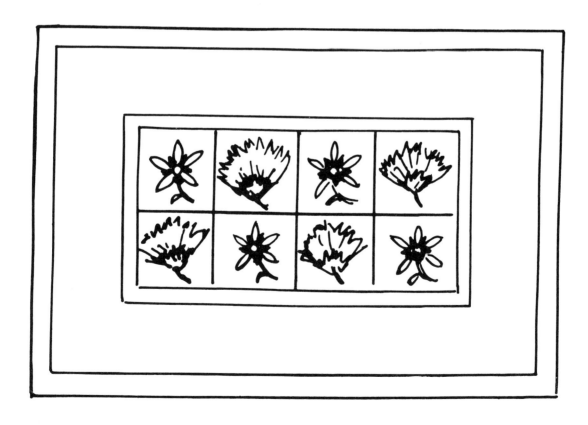

or something more complicated like this:

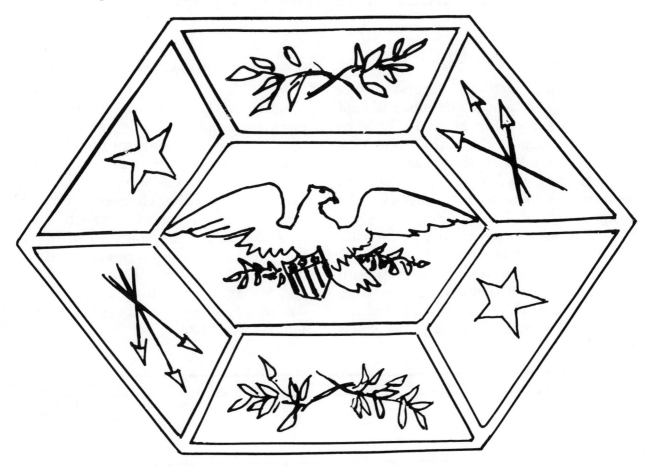

Ideas for rugs are as numerous and varied as you can imagine, but here are some to start you off:

Squares with motifs adapted from children's classics.

Squares devoted to the wildlife and plants common to your area.

Historic scenes, military uniforms, patriotic motifs.

Hobby motifs: Waterfowl for the duck hunter's study, nostalgic railroad engines for the rail buff, butterflies for the lepidopterist, racing cars for the Sunday driver.

Line-for-line copies of wild-animal skins—tiger, leopard, zebra, jaguar—for the conservationist.

Classic European and Oriental rug designs.

Adaptations of patterns from porcelains, folk art, wallpapers, and prints.

A signal-flag border around squares of sailing vessels.

Squares with the great golf holes of the world.

This is a start, and just a start. You'll find information and ideas in hobbyists' magazines, in books, in old

Projects

prints—really anywhere you look.

When you're ready with the design, and prepared to purchase your wool, remember to purchase all background wool from the same dye lot. As you stitch, be careful to keep the canvas as square as possible. It will make it much easier to keep your rug in good condition if you can avoid the necessity of excessive blocking and sizing.

However, blocking for a rug is the same as blocking anything else. The scale is larger, and you might find it advantageous to pin the dampened rug to a piece of old carpet until it has dried thoroughly. If yours is a pieced rug, block each piece carefully to exact dimensions; as each piece dries, put it aside.

If you are going to try doing the piecing yourself, miter the corners, and turn the canvas back so that only a single thread shows all around. Then pin the pieces flat, lined up line for line and mesh for mesh, and join them with your background wool and a curved upholsterer's needle. Where four corners come together, take a single cross stitch.

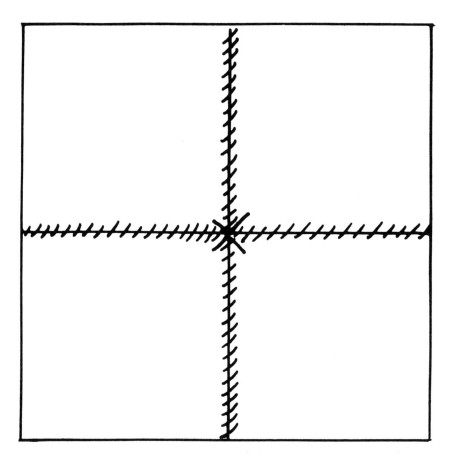

Reinforce your seams with self-sticking rug tape.

Now, add five rows of background around the outside edges; these will be turned under, helping to reinforce your seams. Using two-inch cotton rug tape, hand-sew the tape along the edge of the rug so that it will cover the extra rows of stitching when they are turned back. Once the tape is in place, trim the extra canvas from the piece. Place the rug face down, flat on the floor, and, with a steam iron, turn back the edges, tape and all, pinning them in place as you work. Then sew the free edge of the tape lightly to the back of the rug and steam again. Do not line the rug.

If it is very badly distorted, you may have to glue canvas to the back to keep it in shape, but that is indeed a professional job and should not be tackled at home.

When the rug is thoroughly dry, it should be placed on a good-quality jute pad slightly smaller all around than the rug itself.

UPHOLSTERY

A few words of advice about upholstery:

The only projects that you should attempt yourself are very simple ones, such as covering a dining room chair seat or a footstool. Be cautious about making your pattern even for such simple projects. It is a very good idea to have an upholsterer check your pattern size for you before you begin your stitchery.

To finish a cover for a chair seat or a footstool, simply block and size the piece and leave the excess canvas in place. Attach needlework to the chair seat with nails, being careful to keep the piece perfectly straight. Attach seat to chair and screw in place.

For anything more complex you will have to make up your mind to spend money on the best materials available and the best upholsterer you can find. Have the upholsterer draw the pattern pieces for you, then do your needlework. When you have completed your stitchery, turn the finishing work over to him. Have him put the pieces together with leather welting, which will last as long as your needlework.

Stadium Tote

For football games and such, nothing is handier than this combination tote and cushion. Folded and zipped, it will hold such necessities as a blanket, a picnic lunch, an umbrella, and other odds and ends. Opened and unzipped, it makes a cushion for two.

To make it you'll need a large piece of needlework, 24 inches by 36 inches, canvas or duck lining material that will give you a piece of the same dimensions plus about 10 feet of 1-inch bias strips for ¼-inch bias binding (or commercial bias binding), a piece of 1- to

1½-inch-thick foam rubber the same size as the needlework, about 3 yards of 2-inch canvas webbing the same color as your lining material, thread to match the webbing and lining, invisible thread, and two 14-inch heavy-duty separating jacket zippers.

Lay out your pattern according to the illustration. Design your stitchery to take advantage of the placement of the webbing. Add no continental stitching. Block, size, trim, and reinforce.

Lay out the webbing on the needlework, starting at the fold line, with the end of the webbing folded under. Pin or baste it around to form handles, as indicated on the sketch. Where the webbing joins, turn the ends of the webbing under. Check to make sure that the handles match, and then, with matching thread, edge-stitch the webbing into place, starting one inch from the ends of the needlework, skipping two 4-inch sections on one side of the bag to make a holder for your umbrella, and following the stitching pattern indicated in the sketch. Slip-stitch the ends together.

Now for the lining. Take your lining piece, fold it in half along the fold line, and press. Align your zippers parallel with the edges, the edge of the zipper tape about ¼ inch in from the edge of the lining piece, with the bottom end toward the fold and the top toward the top of the piece. Use masking tape to hold the zippers in place, and check to see that both are perfectly aligned before you sew them in place along the edges, using your zipper foot and matching thread.

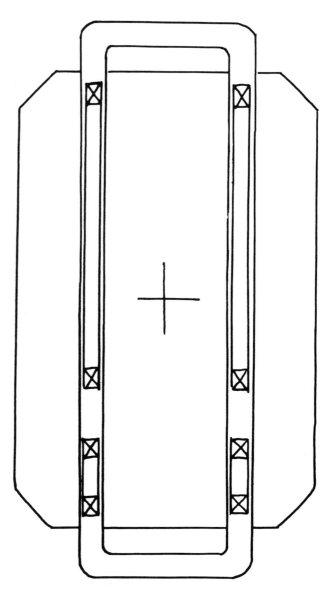

**Carrier, Showing
Placement of Webbing
Straps and Handles**

Projects

If you have not already done so, make your bias binding.

Cut the foam rubber. Make it one inch shorter and one inch narrower than your needlework. Then cut it in two along the fold line and trim away a half inch on the bottom of each half.

Lay your needlework face down. Put the foam-rubber pieces on it, centering them carefully; dab a bit of adhesive on the corners of the foam to hold the pieces in place while you sew. Place the zippered lining piece right side up on top of the needlework and foam. Pin or baste the lining and needlework together, or use masking tape to hold them. Stitch the two pieces together, working close to the edge of the needlework; since the foam is cut a bit smaller, you won't have to stitch through it. Trim excess canvas right next to the needlework; if you've measured carefully, you should not have to trim the lining. Stitch across the center fold line, using invisible thread.

Apply the bias binding, starting on the fold line and continuing all the way around, being careful to keep the handles and zippers out of the way.

Free the handles, connect the zippers, zip them up, and steam the fold line lightly. This is one project that will undoubtedly need a stain-resistant finish. Either spray this on the tote yourself or ask your dry cleaner to apply it. Once you've done that, your all-purpose carrier is ready for its trek to the stadium, racecourse, or whatever.

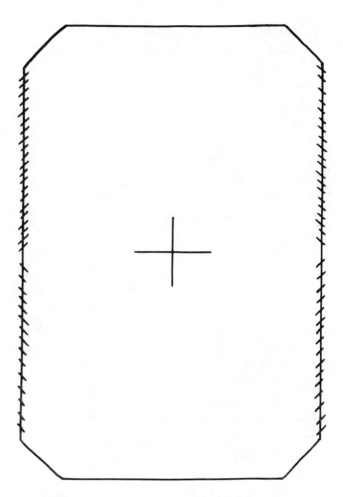

14″-Heavy-Duty Jacket Zippers Positioned on Lining

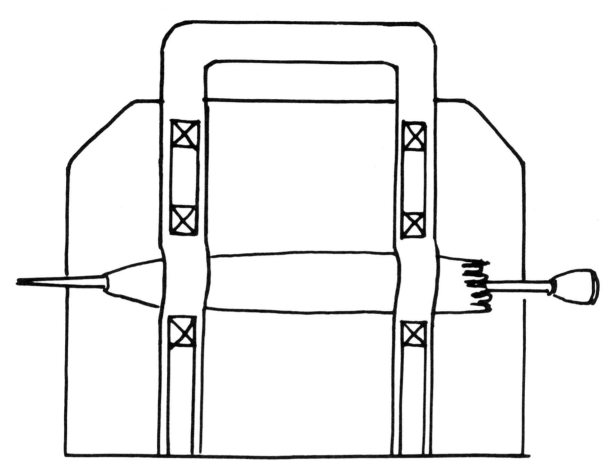

Finished Tote

FOR THE SPORTS-MINDED

There are very few practical things that you can make in needlepoint for the sports buff. Here we give a few suggestions that may help you do something original for your favorite golfer or sailor when Christmas or a birthday rolls around.

There are several sports magazines published for almost every sport you can think of, from golf to sports-car racing. We have found these to be a gold mine of inspiration, particularly if you don't know the first thing about the sport in question. Browse through them and familiarize yourself with the equipment and jargon of the sport, and try to do a design of your own.

Following are some ideas for projects that we like. Most make attractive pillows, small rugs, framed pictures, or coasters. A vest with sporting motifs always makes a great gift—and don't forget the stadium tote for the spectator.

Sailing: 1. A series of signal-flag cushions for the den. If you do cushions for the boat, be sure to do them in synthetic yarn so that they won't mildew.

2. A belt done in signal flags that spell out the name of the boat.

3. Take a photo of the boat and trace it. Have it enlarged photostatically or enlarge it yourself by the graph method. You can then do a line-for-line copy of the craft. Be sure to incorporate the name of the boat in your design.

4. If your sailor is lucky enough to belong to a sailing club, do a design making use of the club's flag or burgee.

Golf: 1. If your golfer has one golf hole that he or she constantly fouls up, get the golf course diagram of that hole showing how to play it in par. You'll have a great design if you make a dotted line for each shot toward par, on a lovely green background, with the flag, the blue sky, and whatever bushes or sand traps are around for color.

2. Take a picture of your golfer swinging his or her club, wearing the appropriate funny hat or looking chic, as you choose. Trace the outline and have it blown up in photostat or enlarge it by the graph method. Transfer it to canvas and do a silhouette of the golfer in this pose. You might try doing the background in a pattern stitch for texture.

3. See the mail-order section of this book for sources of premade golf-club covers.

Tennis: 1. See idea number 2 under "Golf."

2. Make a racket jacket using one of the premade kits available (see mail-order section).

Equestrian: 1. Do our riding-boot design as a pillow or as a Christmas stocking.

2. See idea number 2 under "Golf."

Use these suggestions and apply them to the sport that interests you. With a little bit of luck and imagination and you turn out something wonderful.

Annotated List of Mail Order Suppliers

If you're looking for something specific in your local shops and can't find it, this is the list to consult. It isn't intended to be encyclopedic, but we did try to find at least one source for everything we thought you might be interested in. The emphasis is on prefinished items; you might check through it once to get an idea of the wide range of items available. More come on the market all the time.

If you find that you must write to a manufacturer, tell him where your local craft shop is and who runs it. In this way you'll do the manufacturer a favor by helping him expand outlets for his products, and you'll make it convenient for yourself if something you enjoy working with is available locally.

And while you're at it, if you find a product or service that you like, a shop that does particularly good custom work, or a new technique, please write to us, Pat Feeley and Kathy Archer, % St. Martin's Press, 175 Fifth Avenue, New York, New York 10010. We'll check it out and use it in subsequent editions of this book.

Alice Maynard
724 Fifth Avenue
New York, New York 10019

For over a hundred years this shop has furnished custom needlework and services, including custom design, blocking, and finishing. From cuddly dolls to witty men's slippers, from coasters and director's-chair seats to full-size rugs, they'll execute your idea for you. Their catalog, however, has handsome things available on hand-painted canvas with Persian wool. Not as pricey as it could be, and definitely worth it. Catalog, $1.

Baxwood Crafters
Department M
P. O. Box 7012
Lexington, Kentucky 40502

Exclusive suppliers of handsome, good-quality lamp bases for needlework, in color-coordinated kit form or blank for your own canvas and design. Prompt, courteous service. Catalog.

The Countryside Bazaar
303 South Main Street
Wheaton, Illinois 60187

The retail source for Stitch 'n Learn Needlepoint cards, which are our choice for the best possible instruction in mastering the stitches. Write for information.

Decor Frames
18441 Halsted Street
Glenwood, Illinois 60425

A flexible and genuinely portable needlework frame that will take canvas from less than 12 inches wide to a full 27 inches. To go with it, floor-standing or sit-upon easels. Also Stitch Clean for dry-cleaning your needlepoint. Brochure.

Ellly
P. O. Box 3898-M
New Haven, Connecticut 06525

The specialty here is prefinished items in wide variety—totes and handbags, purse accessories, racket jackets, belts for your waist or collars for Fido's neck, golf-club mittens, magazine racks and planters, even a Christmas stocking, a cover for your typewriter, and a jacket for your *TV Guide*. Also available, wooden items for inserts: game boards, small chairs, footstools, luggage racks. A good line of such things as mesh gauges, inch markers for graphed designs, indelible pens, books, ambidextrous scissors, aids to enlarging. Catalog. Prompt and cheerful service.

Elsa Williams, Inc.
West Townsend, Massachusetts 01474

A joint catalog serves crewel embroiderers and needlepointers alike with handsome and unusual kits of first quality, some on painted canvas and some partially preworked. Nifty rugs, both one-piece and in squares. Excellent selection of canvases, including 5 mesh rug canvas, 13 mesh jute bargello canvas, 13 mesh graph canvas for charted work, and pattern-weave canvas (8 mesh, choice of eight designs). Needlepoint rods, tapestry yarn in a good selection of fine colors, needles, and custom blocking and finishing. Prompt, professional service. Needlework catalog, $1. Sample card for tapestry wool, $1.

A further item of interest is the school conducted here in a handsome old house that once belonged to Winslow Homer. Sessions are each a week long, and they are graded according to level of skill and area of interest. Write for information.

Giftiques Unlimited
P. O. Box 412
Little Neck, New York 11363

Exclusive suppliers of a handsome line of self-mounting desk accessories, including address and engagement books, desk blotters, wastebaskets, cigarette and trinket boxes, telephone-directory covers, and many other items. Also custom finishing on picture frames, door-stopper bricks, and wastebaskets, for which they will supply measurements. Catalog and color samples, $1. First-class merchandise and courteous service.

Jacmore Company
36 West 25 Street
New York, New York 10010

Handbags, evening bags, racket jackets, and purse accessories are among the prefinished specialties here, but the company also has handsome belts for men and women, a dog collar for your pampered pooch, luggage tags and key rings, and a complete line of belt, hand-

bag, and bellpull hardware. Everything's top quality. Good service. Catalog, $1.

Joan Short Originals, Inc.
27694 Camino Capistrano
Laguna Niguel, California 92677

A good selection of kits, including prefinished items such as handbags and purse accessories, belts, sandals, address books, key rings and luggage tags, and so forth. Catalog.

Leatherpoint Creations, Inc.
P. O. Box 171
West Bend, Wisconsin 53095

Handsome, first-quality items in leather and suede with canvas inserts—a full range of purse accessories, and so forth. Write for information.

Meyer Enterprises
Box 644
Sharon, Pennsylvania 16146

The Meyer Needlepoint Blocking Device is large, heavy-duty, and rather difficult to assemble, but it is flexible, taking pieces from 2 × 2 inches to 32 × 32 inches, and sturdy, doing a perfect job on even badly distorted pieces. Once assembled, it can be stored under a bed, ready for use. About $30, at the time of writing, but we think it's worth it. Write for information.

Modern Needlepoint Mounting Company
11 West 32 Street
New York, New York 10001

Custom blocking and finishing for handbags and a wide range of accessories. They'll furnish paper patterns for special items at moderate cost. Brochure.

The Needlecraft Shop
4501 Van Nuys Boulevard
Sherman Oaks, California 91403

Of the available sources this is the best for the basics. Books, charts, transfers, all kinds of canvas and embroidery fabrics, every yarn you can imagine. If you're left-handed, or into petit point, or really looking to expand your skills in stitchery and design, they'll be able to help. Polite service. Leaflet, 25¢; Paterna Persian swatch card, $1; sample swatch of all canvases, $2.50. Much else besides.

The Stitchery
204 Worcester Turnpike
Wellesley, Massachusetts 02181

A fine selection of kits and some prefinished items, usually showing the pick of current designs and mostly of high quality. Prompt, professional service. One-year catalog subscription, 25¢.

The Needleworkshop, Inc.
1601 Arthur Avenue
North Brunswick, New Jersey 089020

Suppliers of "Blockit," an ingenious frame for blocking that does away with pins and takes any size up to 22 by 22 inches. Brochure.

O-P Craft Company, Inc.
425 Warren Street
Sandusky, Ohio 44870

Tissue boxes, boxes for inserts, shadow boxes. These are usually available in craft and hobby shops, but if you can't find what you want, write for catalog.

Sewmakers, Inc.
1619 Grand Avenue
Baldwin, New York 11510

Exclusive suppliers of the perforated card that seems so appropriate for such things as framed mottoes, bookmarks, and so forth. Also frames for needlework handbags. Brochure.

Slantzi-Craft
Stowe, Vermont 05672

The prefinished goods here include many things in denim with inserts, among them a safari jacket, a tennis visor, and an apron. Use washable wools or resign yourself to having the garments dry-cleaned. Catalog.

Sudberry House, Inc.
Colton Road at Exit 71
Box 421
Old Lyme, Connecticut 06371

Attractive objects for inserts, including footstools, small chairs, serving and desk trays, game boards, coasters, trivets, luggage racks, and cheese boards. Retail catalog, $2.

Tandy Leather Company
P. O. Box 2686
Fort Worth, Texas 76101

Stores nationwide. Leathers, leather goods, leather-working tools and fittings, adhesives, clogs—all manner of useful things for the needleworker. Catalog, 25¢, from address above.

Tina of California
1156 North McCadden Place
Los Angeles, California 98038

Kits, but best as a source for prefinished items, including pillows, totes, racket jackets, golf-club mittens, purse accesories, et cetera. Catalog.

Toni Totes of Vermont
South Londonderry, Vermont 05155

The specialty here is canvas totes, prefinished, but in addition you'll find pillows in several styles, belts, racket jackets, leather handbags—all good quality. There's also a nice line of Lucite desk accessories for inserts. Polite, prompt service. Catalog.

BIBLIOGRAPHY

Boyles, Margaret. *American Indian Needlepoint Designs Workbook*. New York: Macmillan Publishing Co., 1976. (Based on material by W. Ben Hunt and J. F. "Buck" Burshears.)

Dover Pictorial Archives Series. Dover Publications, Inc. Dept. DA, 180 Varick Street, New York, N.Y. 10014.

This is a wonderful series that is a great source of design ideas for those of you who like to design your own canvases. They range from snow crystals to musical instruments to Victorian stencils and many more. A catalog is available and the books may also be bought at your local bookstore.

Fischer, Pauline, and Anabel Lasker. *Bargello Magic: How to Design Your Own*. New York: Holt, Rinehart and Winston, 1972.

Has excellent explanatory pictures.

Gartner, Louis J., Jr. *Needlepoint Design*. New York: William Morrow & Co., 1970. A House and Garden Book.

Gladstone, Meredith and Gary. *The Needlepoint Alphabet Book*. New York: William Morrow & Co., 1973.

Grafton, Carol Belenger. *Geometric Needlepoint Designs Charted for Easy Use*. New York: Dover Publications, 1975. $1.50 paperback.

A great buy.

Hanley, Hope. *Needlepoint*. New York: Charles Scribner's Sons, revised and enlarged ed., 1975.

Kaestner, Dorothy. *Four Way Bargello*. New York: Charles Scribner's Sons, 1972.

Kluger, Phyllis. *A Needlepoint Gallery of Patterns from the Past*. New York: Alfred A. Knopf, revised ed., 1975. $15.
Excellent. Contains charts for designs from Egypt up to Early American. A great buy.

Lantz, Sherlee. *Trianglepoint: From Persian Pavilions to OP Art with One Stitch*. New York: Viking Press, 1976. A Studio Book.

————, with diagrams by Maggie Lane. *A Pageant of Pattern for Needlepoint Canvas*. New York: Grosset & Dunlap, second ed., 1975. $15.95.
Very good design ideas, history, and good graphs for patterns.

Lewis, Alfred Allan. *The Mountain Artisans Quilting Book*. New York: Macmillan Publishing Co., 1973.
Many of their design ideas can be applied with great success to needlepoint.

Martin, Mary. *Mary Martin's Needlepoint*. New York: William Morrow & Co., 1969.

Scheuer, Nikki. *Designs for Bargello*. New York: Doubleday & Co., 1973.
Worldwide sources, from antiquity to the seventies, provide the background for 62 bargello designs.

Sidney, Sylvia, and Alfred A. Lewis. *Sylvia Sidney's Needlepoint Book*. New York: Van Nostrand Reinhold Co., 1974.

Williams, Elsa S. *Bargello: Florentine Canvas-Work*. New York: Van Nostrand Reinhold Co., 1976.

Design Your Own Projects

Design Your Own Projects

Design Your Own Projects

Design Your Own Projects